#Charlottesville:

White Supremacy, Populism, and Resistance

Edited by Christopher Howard-Woods,
Colin Laidley, and Maryam Omidi

Public
Seminar
Books

Published by Public Seminar Books in association with OR Books.

© 2018, 2019 Public Seminar Books

The partial reproduction of this publication, in electronic form or otherwise,
is consented to for noncommercial purposes, provided that the original
copyright notice and this notice are included and the publisher and
the source are clearly acknowledged. Any reproduction or use of all or a
portion of this publication in exchange for financial consideration of any
kind is prohibited without permission in writing from the publisher.

Public Seminar Books
79 Fifth Avenue
New York, NY 10003
publicseminar.org

Public Seminar and Public Seminar Books are significant innovations in
academic publishing: slow news and fast books, using the advanced design
and social science resources of the New School. They also flow
out of a deep intellectual-political tradition of the New School and its engagement with the problems of the times and enduring problems
of the human condition: the struggles for cultural freedom and democracy
against tyranny.

Book interior design by Juliette Cezzar

All rights information: rights@orbooks.com

First trade printing 2019

Cataloging-in-Publication data is available from the Library of Congress.
A catalog record for this book is available from the British Library.
ISBN 978-1-949017-00-7 paperback
ISBN 978-1-949017-01-4 e-book

Published for the book trade by OR Books in partnership with Counterpoint Press.
Distributed to the trade by Publishers Group West.

To all who defended democracy at Emancipation Park
on August 11 and 12, 2017.

Table of Contents

Jeffrey C. Goldfarb & Claire Potter

Preface

#CHARLOTTESVILLE is the first in a series to be published by Public Seminar Books, an initiative that expands the digital *Public Seminar* vision to re-imagine and re-constitute the relationship between academic life and the broader public. Knowing that organized, critical perspectives were needed after the events of August 11 and 12, we responded to the urgency of the moment by re-editing essays published over the course of fall 2017, and soliciting several new essays. The horrors of racism vividly and tragically appeared in a particular place, at a particular time, as events of the day, but understanding what happened there then requires confronting enduring problems of the human condition.

We will continue to experiment with content, form, and publishing styles, as we reaffirm and expand the project of the New School for Social Research, and test the limits of what twenty-first century publishing can look like. The mission of *Public Seminar* informs the inquiries here: "confronting the pressing issues of the day and the fundamental problems of the human condition, in open, critical, and challenging ways." This volume is an invitation to continue observing, thinking about, and acting against the legacies of slavery and racism in Charlottesville, in Virginia, in the United States, and far beyond.

—Jeffrey C. Goldfarb and Claire Potter, series editors

Christopher Howard-Woods

Introduction

Before and beyond the tragic events of August 11 and 12, 2017, the town of Charlottesville, Virginia has been best known as the home of the University of Virginia. Founded by Thomas Jefferson in 1819, the university is a UNESCO World Heritage site that possesses some noteworthy artifacts: Moses Ezekiel's 1907 statue of Homer; a section of the Berlin wall with murals by Dennis Kaun; and the Rotunda, the architectural apex of the university's grounds, designed by the founding father himself. A history of the commitment to classical ideas, political engagement, and civic duty is coded into its very landscape. It is known as a "public ivy," a school whose prestige and renown rival the private ivy league, and its esteemed faculty have included philosopher Richard Rorty, Poet Laureate Rita Dove, and astronaut Kathryn Thornton. Charlottesville, in a word, has been to the world a veritable leader in academic pursuits, its community and its campus embodying the highest order of strength of the intellectual spirit.

But on the evening of August 11, Charlottesville came to bear the symbols of an altogether different spirit. White supremacists, in a rally dubbed "Unite the Right," marched in protest of the removal of a statue of Confederate General Robert E. Lee from Emancipation Park, just steps away from the University of Virginia. This removal, a gesture that many municipalities across the country have made towards a more honest recognition of the power of symbols within our nation's troubled past, was especially hard-fought in Charlottesville, where the community has been grappling with Jefferson's own fraught relationship with the institution of slavery and the democratic ideals of his legacy (indeed, what the university and white supremacists have in common is a shared reverence for Jefferson, the latter for his lifelong perpetuation of the lie of biological race, and the former despite it).

Such a reckoning with our history has concerned those among us who consider themselves maligned in the age of political correctness, identity politics, and globalization. The "forgotten men" made themselves known, illuminating their faces by the light of torches, and brought the rest of the country to recognize their insecurity and their rage. As a culture, we are already inclined to obsess over these displays of aggression, but the audacity of the protesters to stake the claim they did made our captivation absolute. Many of us watched in horror. Comparisons were made to Nazi gatherings, and their proclamations ("Jews will not replace us;" "white lives matter") affirmed the motivations and disturbing intent of their action.

The violence, including rioting, beatings, and a fatality, took place within a larger mobilization of white nationalism since the rise of Donald Trump. White supremacists have made themselves more visible by the hospitality of the president's own racist views. Since his election, white supremacist rallies, conferences, and online communities have become more prevalent, and Charlottesville has been their most arresting yet. Photos of the event were shared widely and capture the intensity and spectacle of the gathering: black men lie on the ground, beaten with flag poles and two-by-fours; Confederate and Nazi flags wave above the faces of young white men, distraught and anguished, wearing the signature red hat of the Trump campaign; officers in riot gear press their shields against protesters shouting chants and racial slurs; the flailing bodies of counter-protesters hang delicately in the air as a vehicle rushes through the crowd. Horror led to heartbreak when we learned that this particular action resulted in the death of Heather Heyer. The shock of these images is enduring, and continues to haunt us. We could hardly say we are finished coping with this event. We have barely begun.

Hence, we consider the importance of this book to be evident in, firstly, its robust consideration of the context and implications of this event and, secondly, in its timeliness. It has been less than a year since this event took place, and we are still absorbed in the problems it posed: how do we cope with the political culture that has bred these fraught conditions? How did this despairing ideology proliferate so assiduously? How deep are its roots and to where do they lead? We still seem to be pouring over the statements our political leaders have made, as when the president condemned the violence "on many sides." However, our care to do so is not because such responses offend our delicate political sensibilities. Rather, the "Unite the Right" rally is the consummation of a long history of the systemic oppression of black and brown people; it is the resurgence of a form of hate and violence that finds its precursors in lynchings and in the public burning of crosses. Still, we must acknowledge, it was not a simple reenactment. It is a present day problem and it demands a present day solution.

If the challenges this event poses are numerous and diverse, our responses follow suit. Our deliberation on the organization of the book led us to realize that there was much to be said on topics related to the events of August 2017, and that the structure of this book might do well to divide the direct from the indirect. Thus, you will find that part one includes responses that take up the turmoil of the event explicitly, doing so from various approaches, and part two includes those that provide some context—historical, political, social, and cultural—for the event itself.

Part one begins with vice mayor of Charlottesville Wes Bellamy's account of his experience during the violence and his role as a moral and political leader of the community. Jeffrey C. Isaac, writing in the very first hours of the aftermath, points toward the open question at the heart of so many of the arguments that will follow in this book. Namely, did Trump's rise cause what happened, or was Trump merely an occasion for this hate? Jared Loggins builds on this problematic of white supremacy, asking how the events of Charlottesville signify a failure in the cultural imagination of white Americans. Leonard A. Williams examines how white Ame-ricans typically respond to such criticism through the rhetorical methods of "both-sides thinking" (which Trump was guilty of) and "whataboutism," which appear logical on the surface but hide ideological biases. University of Virginia student Keval Bhatt writes that the covert ideology inherent in the reverence of symbols like Jefferson obfuscates the historical truth of slavery and colonialism. Michael Weinman, in his first of two responses, also observes that the role of slavery in American history is confused, forgotten, or misrepresented.

Following these, Andrew Boyer's response takes up the relationship between violent political action and the slow degradation of our political institutions, demonstrating how habit and pluralism can overcome ideological difference. Isaac Ariail Reed considers the debates around statues, and the legacy of Jefferson in particular, as complex problems in the differences between worldviews, and not simply conflicting means and ends. Gordon Mantler uses two examples of memorials from Washington, D.C. as contrasting paradigms for our political and cultural relation to our fraught past: misleading paternal reverence and the heroism of activism. Laura Goldblatt interrogates how successful the university and police were in protecting the community, questioning who counts as a member of that community in an elite college town. In his second response, Michael Weinman uses Aristotle to help answer the question of whether those who engage in political violence, like the counter-protesters in Charlottesville, are "blameworthy." Maria Bucur borrows from her family's experience in Communist Romania to compare its similarities to authoritarianism and nationalism arising in America today. Part one ends with Reverend Marcus McCullough's frank admission that what happened in Charlottesville was ultimately unsurprising. The United States has repeatedly failed to adequately respond to and account for its dark history of chattel slavery and systemic racism. A gathering of this nature was bound to happen.

Part two includes articles written before and around August 2017 that deal with the political and cultural landscape that led to the violence in Charlottesville. Drawing on Dr. Martin Luther King Jr.'s 1963 sermon on the first black-owned radio station in America, Vaughn Booker begins part two with a denunciation of economic and ethnonationalism. Sanford Schram, sharing these concerns, takes a hard look at the curious ties between the Republican Party and the Russian government—and their shared responsibility for the rise of white nationalism. *Public Seminar*'s Publisher Jeffrey C. Goldfarb argues that "we are still in Charlottesville": how our responses to events in Charlottesville are profoundly affected by the opinions of others in a mediated public sphere that makes us present for the action but isolated from differing opinions. Rachel McKinney analyses the premises of alt-right ideology, arguing that if students of color on American campuses are under increased threat from white nationalist groups, academics could do worse than to become familiar with their ideas.

Public Seminar's Executive Editor Claire Potter reviews the case of Corey Menafee who vandalized a stain-glass window at Yale University depicting a romanticized prewar South, and considers how Confederate public memorials sustain the vitriol of their intended audience. In a joint essay, Nicholas Baer and Maggie Hennefeld offer separate answers to the "post-truth" politics of Trumpism and the alt-right. Baer problematizes Richard Rorty's prescience in the rise of Trump, while Hennefeld looks to Russian author and journalist Masha Gessen's nihilism as a genuine response to the limitations of Enlightenment rationalism.

Melvin Rogers further considers social organization and politics as he examines white supremacy as the genesis of a general "crisis of legitimation"—the perceived failing of democratic institutions for white Americans—which lurks behind the motivations for the "Unite the Right" rally. Drawing on W.E.B. Du Bois's 1890 speech on Robert E. Lee, whose statue precipitated the violence in Charlottesville, Neil Roberts regards America's present dilemma, one precipitated by authority and authoritarianism. Michael Sasha King evaluates different forms of protest against racism and injustice, including San Francisco 49er quarterback Colin Kaepernick's controversial decision to sit during the national anthem. Mitchell Kosters breaks down the constituent logics of white supremacy proper, and considers how they might be further clarified through the concepts of institutions, histories, and spaces. Mindy Fullilove and others take account of the significance of anniversaries, including the upcoming 400th anniversary of the first arrival of enslaved Africans in North America. In a fascinating and painful essay, Julia Ott offers the history of chattel slavery in American economics, from the investment banks like Lehman Brothers that kept the "peculiar institution" afloat to the practice of valuing black bodies as specimens of strength, dexterity, and efficiency. And finally, Eric Anthamatten ends our book with a powerful message about punching Nazis in the face—even if you are categorically against violence, you might still find room for one exception.

The diversity and complexity of these problems call for a reevaluation of our history, our vocabulary, and the terms on which we meet our disputants. We feel the urgency of this need in the daily volley of grim and unfortunate news, the conflicts of a nation still scarred by the stakes over which the Civil War was fought. Perhaps what drives us most to think and rethink through Charlottesville is the deep sense of collective moral failing, that the unbelievable achievements in the last century—including universal suffrage, equality in the workplace and the home, and equal protection under the law, for which lives were lost and ruined and heroes emerged—have been dispossessed by the forces of fear, ignorance, and intolerance. This event is a watershed moment for the apparent rise of white nationalism in America, and we have much to do in order to understand how this came to pass and what it spells for the future. Charlottesville has become a cultural touchstone for those of us who see the era of so-called populism as a threat to the lives of women, people of color, and democracy itself, and we hope to offer this book as one step forward in understanding what has happened and what might come next.

PART 1

Wes Bellamy

The Civil Rights Movement 2.0

A Message from the Vice Mayor of Charlottesville

"We need for everyone to remain in the church until we direct you to do otherwise." Such were the words from the leaders of a church service in Charlottesville, Virginia, on August 11, 2017. There were 500 or so people present, all thinking they were trapped inside, while white supremacists marched outside with tiki torches. Unlike them, we had gathered for an altogether different purpose: a community service about sticking together, standing strong, and how love always overcomes hate. Throughout the service, however, the mood was eerie to say the least. People pretended to show strength and a level of belief that things would be okay, that we had each other's backs ... but that resolve was tested. Throughout the day as well as the days and weeks that led up to August 11, there was a dark cloud looming over the city.

From the barbershops to the city council meetings, in every neighborhood, people were talking about the "Unite the Right" rally on August 12. Being that the leader and organizer of the rally, Jason Kessler, had essentially made it his life mission to try and derail my life and livelihood, people were concerned for my well-being, and the well-being of my family. People were worried not just for me, but for the city as a whole. However for some reason, I was cautiously optimistic that things would be okay. I want to be clear: I am from the Deep South. I have heard countless stories about the KKK, about white supremacists and other groups who despise the color of my skin, doing a variety of hateful and vile things to try and intimidate us. So as I sat in the church, and the news broke that white supremacists were outside with tiki torches, my initial thoughts and feelings made my blood boil. I desperately wanted to fight. I wanted to show that this will not be tolerated, accepted, or allowed in *our* city! I wanted the people in the church to know that things were going to be okay. However, I could do neither. I'm the vice mayor. I can't. I have to remain calm and I have to remain composed.

I was eventually escorted out of the building with the rest of the members of the church to safety, all while nearly 30 or so students from the University of Virginia and the community stood tall and defended the lawn in their own way. They stood up to the white supremacists and let their voices be heard. What they did was incredibly dangerous, some might even say foolish. I call it brave. It was well after midnight when I closed my eyes to go to sleep that I vowed that tomorrow, we would not be intimidated. The hate would not be tolerated.

I woke up on Saturday morning at 4:30 a.m. I prayed and I cried. I felt as if I had spoken to the ancestors. The message was clear: "Stand tall." I told myself that day, I would not feel what I had felt just hours before. We had a sunrise service at the First Baptist Church on West Main Street at 6:00 a.m. As one of the speakers, I arrived a little earlier and met with Cornel West, a philosopher and activist, and one of my heroes. He embraced me and told me he was incredibly proud of me and that the ancestors were as well. I felt his words were divine. The service was electric and empowering to say the least. The mood was different. It felt as if the time to stand up to hate was here. So we marched. I was assigned a security detail of sorts to follow my every move. From the church, myself and others led a march to the historic African American Heritage Center. We then marched from there to the park. We knew what lay ahead of us. We saw the hate in their eyes as we marched, as we chanted, as we stood tall. Our message was clear: "No hate! No fear! White supremacy is not welcome here!" The day was a whirlwind. Some people tried their best to show that our community rejects the notion of hate. Some freedom fighters tried their best. The cowards on the other side took the life of one of our brightest and bravest freedom fighters. They thought she died, but she lives forever. We became stronger together!

Many people have called the days, the weeks, and the months that have followed, "The Awakening." Black people, white people, yellow people, old people, young people, and everyone in between have now seen the hateful ways of the white supremacists who worked to overthrow our city. We have heard from the 45th person to sit in the Oval Office—who I refuse to name—his need to condemn people from "both sides." We heard David Duke, the leader of the Ku Klux Klowns, say that his people came to Charlottesville to fulfill the promise of their president. We saw the hate that some came to our city with. We saw clearly just how they felt about us. We have also seen that we are stronger than they could ever be. For the first time ever, we have since elected an independent to our City Council. For the first time ever, we have two African Americans on our City Council. And, for the first time ever, we have an African American female mayor, my sister Nikuya Walker.

"The Awakening" has been tough for some, painful for others, but necessary for all. We have had City Council meetings in which people have yelled for, and demanded, change. We have seen people throughout our city become more vocal than they have ever been. We have seen a shift. Some have said that this shift, with people being outspoken and expressing their displeasure at City Council meetings and at other venues, is not how we should be conducting ourselves. Yelling, cursing, and being upset scares some people. Some have said that being loud and going about things in that way doesn't get us anywhere. I disagree. We have moved further along in the past four months than we had in the two years I was on the council. In order to get to clean water, you have to go through mud. People deserve to be heard. People deserve to be shown empathy. People have a right to express themselves as they see fit. We all have a responsibility to ensure that things never go back to how they were before. No more covert racism. No more passive aggressiveness. No more holding people back. No more of the old Charlottesville. This is our time. Our time to make this city better, equitable, and free for all. This is the #NewCville.

Wes Bellamy is the vice mayor of Charlottesville, Virginia.

Jeffrey C. Isaac

Charlottesville and Trump

David Duke Explains Neo-Nazi Violence to You

There is fire and fury today on the streets of Charlottesville, Virginia.

Neo-Nazis and white supremacists, some bearing guns, are violently protesting the removal of a statue of Robert E. Lee and attacking anti-racist counter-protesters.

David Duke has declared that this is President Donald Trump's vision for America.

"We are determined to take our country back," Duke said from the rally, calling it a "turning point." "We are going to fulfill the promises of Donald Trump. That's what we believed in. That's why we voted for Donald Trump, because he said he's going to take our country back."

Duke was a neo-Nazi/racist long before Trump became a political figure. He is no doubt seeking to exploit this situation. More importantly, he is stoking embers and flames of white racial and racist resentment that have a long contemporary history (the Civil Rights Act of 1964) and a much longer history (slavery, Jim Crow, structures of institutionalized racism that persist into the present). What is happening today in Virginia is not due to "Trump," and combating both right-wing extremism and underlying structures of racism, and also the structures of economic dislocation that generate a politics of resentment, requires much more than criticizing Trump.

AT THE SAME TIME, electoral politics matters, and executive politics matters, and these are not mere "expressions" of underlying social and economic causes. Trump ran an extremist, right-wing populist and xenophobic campaign against the political establishment in general. His campaign centered on mobilizing white racism and resentment and normalizing and legitimizing the so-called alt-right. As president he has installed a set of powerful far-right figures—Steve Bannon, Michael Flynn, Sebastian Gorka, Stephen Miller, the crank who wrote the NSC memo—at the highest reaches of political power, many in the White House. He has actively attacked all establishment media in favor of Breitbart-style "truth." He has regularly employed violent rhetoric about his opponents. He has invited violence against protesters and encouraged police violence against suspects. He has vilified Black Lives Matter. Trump has done all of this and more. And so Duke is not "wrong" when he claims to be "true" to the Trump agenda. Because Duke, Richard Spencer, and the rest, have been encouraged, mobilized, and normalized by Trump.

To that extent, it is impossible to understand, and to combat, what is happening right now in Charlottesville, without recognizing the danger that Trump and Trumpism pose to social justice and to liberal democracy.

Saying this is not "hysterical" or "tyrranophobic." And it does not reduce everything to Trump, or insist that other dynamics and institutions are not also responsible. In my opinion saying this is a precondition of serious political analysis right now. There are other things worth saying too. But to avoid this is, I am afraid, mistaken.

Jeffrey C. Isaac is James H. Rudy professor of political science at Indiana University, Bloomington. Originally published on Public Seminar, *August 12, 2017.*

Jared Loggins

Loss Beyond Destruction

Charlottesville Reveals the Failures of Loss

Just after midnight on New Year's Day in 2006, a neighbor comes banging on the door of the apartment my parents rented in Memphis.

"Get out, get out," the person screams, the space in between the bangs growing closer and closer together as the warning continued.

The apartment building is on fire. My brother, my parents, and I are all home and luckily we are able to hear the warning. We gather some essential possessions and leave. Not wishing for either of us to lose any more sleep, my parents whisk my brother and me around the corner to a family member's house. He and I stay put for the night.

The following morning my parents arrive to drive us back to the house. Everything is gone. Everything. Local news cameras were on the scene, as a person—a neighbor—died that night in the fire. We also lost our cat.

A loss of this magnitude is unimaginable until it happens. The feeling is mostly grief. After all, this was the place of so many memories. The loss was followed by reckoning. How was I to move forward having lost a home filled with irreplaceable memories? And how was I to go about filling the void without descending into madness?

I recently reflected on this as I moved into a new apartment and attempted to appraise the value of my possessions for a renter's insurance application. I can very clearly and for the most part accurately quantify the cash value of my possessions; I cannot, however, fully account for the meaning of their potential loss.

The memories enclosed in things and other living beings—if those things and beings matter to us—hold something beyond monetary value. We are psychically attached to them. Perhaps we can reckon with losing them, but we certainly cannot render a full account of how the losses might transform us in advance of their loss. Nor can we fully replace that which has gone. That loved one or loved thing held a special place, we might say. On this measure, we will have to choose whether or not our psychic attachments to things, identities, ourselves can be undone in order to make room for others in the wake of loss. We will have to decide whether we have the sufficient will to handle loss without becoming jaded.

Why do we struggle so? Could it be that we believe we cannot go on in the world without that which is gone or that, somehow, losing those things means we also become unrecognizable to ourselves?

The most recent iteration of this struggle comes in a twisted and perverse form. The scene that has unfolded in Charlottesville is vile and evil. White supremacists, a title fast becoming demographically unviable though still institutionally affirmed, descended on the town to protest the removal of a confederate monument in honor of the losing side's General Robert E. Lee. But the stakes for them seem higher than this.

"One nation, one people, one immigration," they are said to have chanted, marching onto the campus of University of Virginia with their bamboo torches and khaki pants. The removal of the statue that animates their immediate cause is but a proxy for their real grievance: they are losing their grip on power. If this grievance seems to reflect the appearance of a fringe, alt-right sentiment, that would betray the litmus test on which far too many white Americans hedged their bets in 2016: new data from the Public Religion Institute identified, somewhat euphemistically, "cultural anxiety" as one of the primary reasons many voters pulled the lever for Trump.

Trump voters believe their world is collapsing, their identities being crushed by a burgeoning multicultural society. And so they lash out.

Physically, they unleash their terror on the innocent as was the case when a homeless man was violently beaten in Boston in May 2015; or when two men were brutally murdered in Portland in an anti-Muslim attack in early 2017. In Charlottesville, their lashing out produced three casualties, and 19 serious-to-critical injuries according to the Virginia State Police.

Rhetorically, they peddle dog-whistles and racist stereotypes about people of color: like the whopping 45 percent of Republicans who think black people make up the majority of welfare recipients; or when Trump himself told a crowd of his supporters during Black History Month that black youth "have no spirit."

Some of this is no doubt the immediate consequence of an administration that has used all its resources to trample over the values of a pluralistic society. But this is also a gross failure of individual and collective imagination. The "culturally anxious" white Americans who put Trump into the Oval Office mostly fail at undoing their psychic attachments to unearned privilege in the face of the competing visions of freedom, justice, and equality.

The shadow of Ferguson and the new era of black activism that has grown in its wake offers a moment to reflect. Black Americans facing down police violence on the streets and in the political domain regularly come up against loss. There is the loss of life that instigates the protests in the first instance. The unrelenting news reports of premature deaths of black Americans due to state violence are a reminder of systematic disregard. But there is also the failure to get justice—a failure that has the potential to hobble our efforts, to disempower us from continuing to go forward. Why bother, we ask? Yet, we have continued onward. Loss has not become ruin and destruction. There are no dead who can be genuinely claimed to be the result of our crumbling in the face of loss. No bitterness can be claimed to have weakened our resolve.

The same cannot be said of those who've looked on, inspired by Trump as he ascended to the White House under the banner of rage and resentment. For more than a year, they sneered in fake concern at his rallies as he lectured them about what little black and Latino voters had to lose by electing him; at times, cajoling him as he encouraged violence against dissenters. They had everything to lose, we now know.

Political theorist Danielle Allen argues in her book *Talking to Strangers* that democratic politics demands that those who face loss must nonetheless accede to it. In other words, they must not lose sorely. The unjustified resentment of many of Trump's supporters—in its physical and rhetorical forms—offends this principle and another. Democratic politics also demands that we share, equitably. Failing to do either, both Trump voters and the fringe from which they now wish to run become the paradigmatic example of sore losers—stingily decrying liberal welfare statism as the exclusive tool of greedy minorities. Unable to now offer the periodic self-appraisal that equality demands, unable to loosen their attachments to an oppressive form of whiteness, that feeling of losing now descends into madness. The deluded version of sacrifice is tyranny and violence is its expression.

The difficult question the polity must now work out is whether we can stay with the loss of a world without descending into madness; whether our pre-existing attachments can be undone in order to make room for another reality, perhaps a more just one. Will white Americans be capable of losing psychic attachments to unjust privileges? Can they reckon with substantive equality without identifying it with tyranny and oppression?

Whether or not any of this is possible depends on our collective imagination in the face of this terrible set of circumstances. Wherever we go, we are going together.

Jared Loggins is a Ph.D. candidate in political science (political theory and American politics) at Brown University. Originally published on Public Seminar, *August 17, 2017.*

Leonard A. Williams

On Trump's Response to Charlottesville

Political Encounters and Ideological Evasions

The recent clashes involving "Unite the Right" protesters and counter-protesters in Charlottesville, Virginia, cost Heather Heyer her life. Her death and President Donald Trump's response to it have dominated the news of late.

To recount the salient events, fighting broke out between "Unite the Right" protesters (a group of white nationalists, white supremacists, neo-Nazis, and others associated with the alt-right) and counter-protesters (who oppose white supremacy and fascism, including members of the antifa or anti-fascist movement). One right-wing protester deliberately drove a car into a crowd of counter-protesters, killing Heather Heyer. In response to the tragedy, the president spoke first of the bigotry and violence "on many sides," and then reversed course to call out neo-Nazis and others for their disreputable beliefs a couple of days later. He subsequently returned to his original message of blaming both sides in his press conference the following day.

People have said and written so much about these matters that I hesitate to offer yet another take. What compels me to write, though, is a sense that our reactions to this event and others often go awry. We are frequently caught between a cultural tendency to seek the middle ground in any conflict and a political environment that regards an opponent as totally wrong, if not morally evil. In this context, Trump both reflects and embodies two widespread, flawed styles of political discourse: "both-sides thinking" and "whataboutism."

Beginning with "both-sides thinking": blaming both sides in any conflict obviously asserts a degree of equivalence between the words or actions of the implicated groups. You attribute blame in this way usually when you want to avoid some challenge to your own credibility. It is a way of saying that, no matter what your opponent thinks, you have an even-handed position. You seemingly apply the same standard to all comers, suggesting that you are not siding with one team over another.

This seems to be the rhetorical impulse behind Trump's statements about the events in Charlottesville. No fair-minded person would accuse him of backing white supremacists if they turned out to be just as hateful and violent as a group of "anarchists" on the front lines of the antifa crowd. For people to suggest otherwise simply proves that they have been cowed by political correctness or deluded by the purveyors of fake news.

Why is it both easy and comforting to blame both sides in a conflict? It is easy because we have been taught that the way to be fair-minded is to avoid falling into the trap of "either/or" by instead embracing a "both/and" approach. It is comforting because we can portray ourselves as noncombatants, as neutral arbiters. In politics, sometimes one side is more at fault, or is more in tune with cherished values, than the other is. The reflexive blaming of both sides thus ignores context; it obscures the motives and goals of the participants. One stays above the fray only by failing to make a choice.

"Whataboutism" takes two forms. One form emerges when you think you have found a hole in your opponent's position. You suspect that they are guilty of some hidden hypocrisy or logical error that you need only expose by a pointed and poignant question. The other form emerges when you seek to deflect criticism or blame. It functions as a deft move to change-the-subject. Someone accuses you of doing something bad. You respond with a quick, "What about the bad thing you do?"

Both forms appeared in a single exchange during a February 2017 interview with Trump on Fox News. In response to the president's professed respect for Russian President Vladimir Putin, Bill O'Reilly tellingly observed, "Putin is a killer." Trump replied, "There are a lot of killers. You got a lot of killers. What, you think our country is so innocent?"

Indeed, Trump used a similar approach in response to the events in Charlottesville. If you think the alt-right is bad, then what about the alt-left? As he noted in an August 15 press conference, "You had a group on one side that was bad and you had a group on the other side that was also very violent."

At first glance, changing the subject, or calling attention to another's defects, rightly broadens political conversation by raising vital issues that might go unexamined. However, a moment's reflection reveals that the aim of the "whataboutist" is not to begin a comprehensive inquiry. The goal is to absolve oneself of responsibility. By asking "what about ...?" you force others to look at what seems to be the big picture. Really, though, all you seek is to get out of a political or logical pickle, to avoid authentic self-examination.

As forms of political discourse, "both-sides thinking" and "whataboutism" emerge from the same source—an encounter with an adversary or opponent whose worldview is different from one's own. Difference is common, but the problem is that we often treat difference as symptomatic of a skewed, mistaken view of the world. Something is wrong with the other, and that something is ideology.

In such encounters, one's goal is not to understand or empathize with the opponent. The goal is to win the argument by raising uncomfortable questions, by challenging the moral worth of the opponent, by poisoning the enemy with words. When you engage in "both-sides thinking" or "whataboutism," you seem logical and rational on the surface, but you really aim to avoid responsibility or to mount an attack. Political discourse of this sort is not rooted in genuine conversation. Its appearance masks the reality of ideological bad faith—not being willing to admit that one is over-simplifying complex political events and judgments, and doing so in the service of partisan beliefs and interests.

Understanding these features of today's political discourse will neither usher in the Age of Aquarius nor make America great. However, it will help us navigate the conversations that will arise when the next street fight becomes a semiotic one.

Leonard Williams is dean of the college of education and social sciences and professor of political science at Manchester University in North Manchester, Indiana. Originally published on Public Seminar, *August 25, 2017.*

Keval Bhatt

Subverting the Symbols of White Supremacy

The Wolf and the Fox

Content warning: graphic violence, death.

Fascism had always seemed to me a thing of the past. It was almost like a fairy-tale I was told—a passive deterrent, an unreal warning—while going through school. But school was not my education; my real education occurred as I entered the fight against fascism in the modern world, or, more accurately, as the fight was forced upon me. And so, the position I find myself in now is a position I stumbled into. I tripped into a chasm that had been obscured from me during my childhood and adolescence. I was not ready.

I attend the University of Virginia in Charlottesville, Virginia, a city that has drawn the attention of the entire world due to the scarred, beaten, and burned students who stood against white nationalists, white supremacists, and fascists bearing torches on the night of August 11 and due to the horrific murder that occurred on August 12. It has been two months since those horrifying two days—two months of attempts at healing; two months of attempts at understanding; two months of attempts at fighting.

The process of healing from, understanding, and fighting the germinating seed of the overt white supremacist movement in what I hoped would be my home drove me and a group of students at the university to address what surrounds the seed: the soil that allows for the violence of fascism and white supremacy to grow and pervade our "modern" society. This hidden soil is the foundation that the United States is built on, a foundation laid by the founding fathers we, as a nation, so fervently revere. A group of students and I—hand-in-hand with faculty, clergy, and active community members—in mourning and commemoration of the victims of the battle waged in August, shrouded the statue of one of the most lauded founding fathers: one of the authors of the Declaration of Independence, the founder of the university I attend, the slave-master and colonizer, Thomas Jefferson. This action was, at its core, purely symbolic and in no way caused any physical damage. The university administration, however, saw the shrouding as a "desecration of sacred ground," a profane assault on the image of the university's benevolent father. Before I go into this, though, I must tell you of the wolf and the fox, an analogy that is useful in understanding the climate for oppressed peoples and invokes the thought of Malcolm X.

Though they both hunt lamb, the wolf and the fox use different methods to hunt their prey: one overt and openly violent, the other more covert and sinister. The wolf hunts the lamb combatively: snarling and ruthless, it chases the lamb in the open fields and devours it before the whole world. The fox, however, is more cunning in its hunt of the lamb. The fox shows its teeth as the wolf does but in such a way that it seems to be smiling. The fox seems a friend to the lamb, and it waits for the lamb to approach as a friend before it makes its kill.

Malcolm X originally painted this picture to outline the relationship of oppressed people of color to the wolfish political "conservative" and the fox-like political "liberal." I draw it in a similar sense: to invoke the different violent natures of outright white supremacy—marching through a university campus with torches, chanting "white lives matter" and "Jews will not replace us," and driving a car into a crowd of anti-fascist protesters—and systemic oppression, present-day slavery in the form of the prison-industrial complex, gentrification, and capitalism itself, especially the hyper-capitalist neoliberal economy of the modern world. Symbols of the wolf, such as the multitude of Confederate statues, have rightfully come under attack, but the symbols of the fox pervade every part of Western society. The very institution of our republic is a monument to the fox. The brutality of the wolf makes the "gentle" nature of the fox seem an ideal alternative. However, the two are both inherently oppressive and cannot exist without one another.

Our republic, designed by the founding fathers, is predicated on the limited understanding of freedom and liberty that is the basis of liberal philosophy. The notion of rights endowed at birth that cannot be taken away is a noble one, but as the implementation of liberal practice in politics and economics has demonstrated since its introduction into modern political organization, this notion is never without exceptions. At the beginning of our republic, the very idea of natural rights was a fantasy for people of color, those deemed under the law of our great republic to be inhuman property. The American republic is built on land taken through one of the most successful genocides in human history. Where was the right to life, liberty, and the pursuit of happiness for the natives, or the slaves, or the proletarians who had no property but their commodified ability as workers? These were not the persons Jefferson wrote for—indeed they were not considered full persons and thus not part of the republic. The systems of slavery and private property, then, are presupposed in the republic and those very systems are epitomized in our lofty and highly fetishized symbols of said republic. Jefferson, one of the faces carved into hills sacred to indigenous peoples, and the University of Virginia, a school that has consistently dehumanized workers of color and allowed—under the guise of upholding liberal values—white supremacy to fester within its walls, must be addressed as symbols that give white supremacy legitimacy as a movement. There is a reason that Richard Spencer and Jason Kessler, both well-known white supremacists, are obsessed with making the University of Virginia the new capital of white supremacy and fascism in the Western world. It is because the fetishization of Jefferson and the liberal republic has led to the fetishization of values and institutions that have served white supremacy for 200 years.

To combat the wolf, we must combat the fox. Our world is structured by institutions of hierarchy and inequality, and it is through these very institutions that the fox can devour the lamb. Prisons everywhere are being filled with the poor, the impoverished, and people of color; in their sheer size our prisons rival the Soviet gulags, yet in our moral assessment of our prisons we rationalize their inherent oppression and brutality as a necessity, a "peace" predicated on unjust violence. Everywhere neighborhoods predominantly populated by people of color are being invaded by the privileged and the affluent, increasing rents and forcing those same people of color out of their homes and onto the streets—another form of structural, material violence. Health care is being taken away. Undocumented peoples are continually being stripped of their humanity. Labor is as alienating as it has always been. Life, liberty, and the pursuit of happiness remains a fantasy for people of color, for queer and trans people, and still for the whole of the proletariat. To combat the fox we must combat liberalism, capitalism, and our very republic that upholds these unjust conditions. This is why I helped with the shrouding: to attack the symbols of both the wolf and the fox. This is why I take part in every action I can at this university that makes the gruesome reality of people of color known to my peers and the world, as much as my peers and the world may twitch at the thought of their fetishized idol being desecrated.

As a student of the university and a member of the Charlottesville community, it's not only my responsibility but my imperative to communicate to my fellow community members what these symbols mean and what it means to subvert them. The Charlottesville community cannot afford to keep idolizing a man who perpetuated racism and dehumanization, nor can it afford to keep being subjected to a hierarchy that puts profit over its well-being and continues to be the bringer of destruction for the community. Capitalism and the way the university treats its community is the source of this destruction. The university administration and the Charlottesville city government have failed to serve and benefit the community, and frankly, they always will. A world predicated on capitalism and exploitation will never be free from oppression and the oppressed will never be free. We need a future devoid of idolatry, devoid of hierarchy, and devoid of the institutions that allow violence against oppressed people to exist. We need freedom now lest it become impossible in the future. This is a call for solidarity and action from those who have been too passive in the rise of fascism in the United States. We need a different collective understanding of the world we live in, and we must act on that understanding. The time for discussion and passivity is rapidly coming to an end, and those who live under the heavy boot of oppression can't get out from under it by themselves.

I keep asking myself questions in the wake of the infancy of my fight against fascism: how close are we to the fall of the republic? How close are we to the abolition of capitalism and injustice? How close are we to the revolution that I yearn for? These questions have always come after the one that has frightened me most: are we ready? I fear, considering the ubiquity of the republic and the symbols that foster white supremacy, we will stumble, trip into the chasm of fascism as the world once did. I fear that, as I have been unready for this threat to my existence and the existence of my closest friends and family, the world will not be ready for what is to come.

Keval Bhatt currently attends the University of Virginia in Charlottesville, where they are pursuing a B.A. in philosophy and a B.A. in sociology. Originally published on Public Seminar, *October 17, 2017.*

Michael Weinman

Learning from Charlottesville Before and After "Unite the Right"

Misrepresentation, Misrecognition, and
Statue Politics

The first four months of the presidency of Donald Trump were replete with "teachable moments." These centered on tone-deaf comments from high-ranking members of the administration (such as Betsy DeVos, US secretary of state, and Ben Carson, US secretary of housing and urban development) reflecting America's struggle to make sense of the legacy of slavery. In October 2017, the president's chief of staff, John Kelly, claimed that "an inability to compromise" rather than slavery caused the Civil War. This statement, and the responses thereto, makes clear that popular discourse today is no less confused on slavery's distinctive role in American history than before the conflagrations of white supremacy and ethnonationalism in Charlottesville in August 2017. In what follows, I return to the brief spike of interest in the historical singularity of chattel slavery and its aftermath in American politics during the winter of 2017 in order to shed light on the events of August 11 and 12 in Charlottesville. In so doing, I suggest that the incapacity to come to terms with the historical misrepresentation of those who were subjected to chattel slavery is constitutive of the continuing incapacity for many persons of good faith to understand what is at stake in the statue politics that boiled over this summer. This is a historical misrepresentation that will continue so long as we fail to come to terms with chattel slavery as an integral part of America's (at best) disjointed path toward equality and freedom.

THE HISTORICAL MISREPRESENTATION OF SLAVES AS IMMIGRANTS

On February 27, 2017, DeVos issued a public statement that said Historically Black Colleges and Universities (HBCUs) "are real pioneers when it comes to school choice," and "are living proof that when more options are provided to students, they are afforded greater access and greater quality. Their success has shown that more options help students flourish." The next day she tried to distance herself from the implication that her statement was intended, as some pithily put it, to whitewash the history of slavery and segregation in the face of which the HBCUs were created. The impression nevertheless remained.

A week later, on March 6, Carson waded into similarly troubled waters when he claimed: "That's what America is about. A land of dreams and opportunity. There were other immigrants who came here in the bottom of slave ships, worked even longer, even harder for less. But they, too, had a dream that one day their sons, daughters, grandsons, granddaughters, great-grandsons, great-granddaughters might pursue prosperity and happiness in this land." Facing immediate outrage from many quarters—including a sharp statement from the Anne Frank Center—Carson (unlike DeVos) defended his controversial words, saying: "I think people need to actually look up the word immigrant. Whether you're voluntary or involuntary, if you come from the outside to the inside, you're an immigrant. Whether you're legal or illegal, you come from the outside to inside, you're an immigrant. Slaves came here as involuntary immigrants but they still had the strength to hold on."

Carson is wrong—and I have looked the word up, as he might also want to—but before we get into that, I'd like to step back from the immediate, partisan context of these two gaffes. I'd like to suggest that they are symptomatic of something far more nefarious than misrepresenting the degradations and dehumanization to which people of color in the United States have been subjected (Which, don't get me wrong, is bad enough.) What is truly telling about these two moments is how, individually and collectively, they build upon a notion—a wrong-headed and demonstrably false notion—that American society somehow entered a "post-racial" moment with the election of former President Barack Obama. That Obama himself, while always careful not to endorse this notion, contributed to its proliferation in his words and deeds, does not exonerate DeVos and Carson. But that fact does contextualize their errors, telling us something we still need to face about how hard it really is for Americans of all ideological temperaments and of all races to come to terms with the past.

The rhetoric used by Obama during his two-term presidency bears on what made it possible for Carson to say something as outrageous as he did. Indeed, as the far-right media platform *Breitbart News* first reported, and which was later picked up by various outlets both expressly partisan and non-partisan, Carson's claim bears a close resemblance to something Obama said in December 2015 during a naturalization ceremony at the National Archives: "So life in America was not always easy. It wasn't always easy for new immigrants. Certainly, it wasn't easy for those of African heritage who had not come here voluntarily, and yet in their own way were immigrants themselves. There was discrimination and hardship and poverty. But, like you, they no doubt found inspiration in all those who had come before them. And they were able to muster faith that, here in America, they might build a better life and give their children something more." Strongly similar, no doubt. What's interesting about that?

I cannot know and will not know what was in the minds and hearts of enslaved persons on the ships that carried them against their will to a life of involuntary servitude thousands of miles away from the land of their ancestors. But, having read slave narratives—which themselves have their own ideological distortions—and being not entirely unfamiliar with the careful studies that have been done on chattel slavery in America and the Americas, I find this statement from Obama to ring false. But let's put that to the side. Whether or not human beings, sent in chains across the ocean, held hope in their hearts or not, and whether or not "they found inspiration in all those who had come before" (here, if I am not mistaken, it seems Obama has shifted from speaking of persons who were captured or bought in Africa and shipped across the ocean to speaking of their descendants), the important claim in this quote from Obama is what came before, when he says: "... yet in their own way [they] were immigrants themselves."

Here we see the crucial overlap between Obama's claim and Carson's defense of his claim: slaves "in their own way" were immigrants. Here, Obama is wrong, and so is Carson. And it is a meaningful wrongness. Let me try to say why, as I see it. Persons who are trafficked against their will are not immigrants. Every immigrant is someone who was first an emigrant, and in order to be either, a person needs to be a migrant. But migrancy connotes moving and, crucially, the freedom of movement, and such freedom of movement is a key constituent of, and contributor to, personhood. Having personhood means being the sort of entity that can act with intention, for instance to move to (to migrate), to move away from one place (to emigrate), and toward another (to immigrate). Trafficked persons, like the enslaved Africans both Carson and Obama exhort us to imagine on those boats on the Atlantic, were deprived of that personhood and thus, that capacity to move. This might sound abstract, but they were literally deprived of their freedom to move. Not figuratively, but literally, physically deprived. This freedom of movement was denied and, unlike a prisoner or someone else who was considered to have had their person "confiscated," an enslaved person was deprived of that personhood without hope of restoration. This is not a metaphor: this is cold historical reality.

Why does this matter so much? It matters because it displays our incapacity to see enslaved persons—especially those who were captured and shipped across the ocean, but also their descendants—as persons who were deprived of their personhood. We want so badly to redeem American history and our cultural and political heritage that we blind ourselves to what is irredeemable in that past. No, enslaved persons were not immigrants. Precisely because they were not immigrants I consider it immoral for us to fantasize about what "hopes and dreams" or what "inspirations" they might have had. Why? I know we are being asked to engage in this fantasy as an act of moral imagination that restores the basic humanity of those persons "in the bottom of slave ships" as Carson put it. I don't doubt that he means the exercise to be empowering, and I don't disagree that Obama's speech had the same intended effect. I respect their efforts, but I also find them to be, in actual effect, immoral. The immorality rests in our willingness to believe that America is and was the "land of opportunity," the place where, among other things, HBCUs could be "pioneers in school choice."

We must shout "NO!" at this whole line of thought and educate ourselves about the harsh realities of American history. We need, in short, to be honest with ourselves and with our children. And we need our leaders to lead the way. We need them to call upon us, first and foremost, to face and to retell the *hard* history of how the practice of chattel slavery deprived enslaved persons of the very conditions that make having hopes and dreams possible. We need to recall that at the most basic level to be enslaved was to lack a future, as well as a present and a past. Yes, even the kind of temporality that makes personhood possible was deprived to enslaved persons. We need to teach and remember that the crimes of the past were so basic and so thoroughgoing that their legacy outlives (not outlived) them, even as we all, regardless of ideology, aspire to an America that is truly free of that legacy of unfreedom.

What exactly does this have to do with white supremacy and the "Unite the Right" rally in Charlottesville? The link becomes clear if we turn to comments delivered by Representative Steve King (R-Iowa) in March 2017 intended—along with attempts by DeVos and Carson, and more recently Kelly—to whitewash the extent to which chattel slavery was implicated in the development of the American republic. King made a series of increasingly inflammatory comments about the need to protect "our civilization"—by which he meant either or both "Western" or "American" civilization—from the influence of "someone else's babies," apparently indicating immigrants, specifically from the Middle East. But then, as CNN reported,[1] King clarified

---

1   Chris Massie, "Steve King: Blacks and Hispanics 'will be fighting each other' before overtaking whites in population," *CNN*, March 14, 2017.

that what he meant was that the cultural contributions of white Americans are under threat. He also stated his prediction that the white population will remain the majority in the United States because "Hispanics and the blacks will be fighting each other." King defended his view to Chris Cuomo in a CNN interview: "This is an effort on the left, I think, to break down the American civilization and the American culture and turn it into something entirely different. I'm a champion for Western civilization …There are civilizations that produce very little [freedom], if any. This Western civilization is a superior civilization, and we want to share it with everybody."[2]

These statements are not mere misstatements but rather immoral acts. This is so, I would claim, because misrepresentation today— even when done in the service of upholding moral principles such as the dignity of the person and the equality of all people before the law—can never correct past misrecognition. More than that, when we attempt to cast back our "correct" recognition of person or persons who were *mis*recognized in the past, we actually commit a further immoral act by refusing to do justice to the past, as well as to that person or those persons who had injustice done to them in the past. Worse yet, we underwrite the assumptions that bring about further misrecognitions today. The misrecognition of enslaved persons during the period of the transatlantic slave trade has a direct link to the misrecognition of minorities today. More starkly, errors of judgment like those from Obama and Carson about the nature of slavery make it possible (though surely not obvious or necessary) for a view like King's to be articulated as a serious defense of "American culture." Most members of polite

2   Theodore Schleifer, "King doubles down on controversial 'babies' tweet," *CNN*, March 14, 2017.

society and many politicians of both parties will decry King's statements. That is good and right. But are they ready to see the ways in which the discourse about American exceptionalism and our inability to reckon fully with our past make his point of view plausible?

If there's any merit to this analysis of misrepresentation and misrecognition, then what is to be done so that our history (our "cultural heritage") is not misrepresented by the likes of King for the sake of further current misrecognitions? First, we must stress that we judge rightly when we recognize today that *of course* enslaved Africans were persons, and as persons must surely have had hopes and dreams, inspirations and aspirations—that is, that they had dignity. But we must go on to say that this must be so because as persons, those Africans whose personhood was confiscated along with their freedom of movement, were and are equal to each and any of all us as persons. Let us pause here to note that this misrecognition of Africans as non-persons also has a history.[3] Most of us likely don't know that in the early colonial period, Africans were considered indentured servants *just like indentured servants from Europe.* They were persons, whose labor was the property of their master for a set period of time, after which they were free to sell their labor as they chose. Africans came to be misrecognized as non-persons, as "slaves," only after a precedent was set (in 1654 or 1655) through a suit brought by an African who had become a free man, named Anthony Johnson. Johnson successfully claimed that his African servant, John Casor, and not Casor's *labor* was his property. As Kat Eschner notes in a recent piece for the Smithso-

---

3 Ariana Kyl, "The first slave," *Today I Found Out,* August 23, 2013.

nian blog,[4] this decision became settled law by 1671 in Virginia and spread from there to the colonies at large. As property, enslaved persons were no different from sugar, gold, spice, grain, cotton, or any other inanimate cargo.

With this history in mind, while it is fundamentally right-minded that we wish to attribute our judgment and our correct recognition of Africans as full persons back to the time of the transatlantic slave trade, it is fundamentally wrongheaded to state as actual fact, that those enslaved persons had that personhood. And we are doubly wrong when we suggest that in addition to such personhood they also experienced the recognition that makes it possible, first, to do incredibly basic things like move freely, and then to do something like wish, hope, or plan for the future. That wrongheadedness, when based on ignorance, is an error to be forgiven, or if not forgiven, pitied. But when, as with the statements of Obama and Carson, the error is based on a willful distortion of the past, then what is forgivable or pitiable becomes an immoral offense. For such willful distortion is a conscious *misrepresentation* of the past that cannot and will not correct the *misrecognition* of Africans as non-persons in the past.

Why consider the details of these depravities? One important reason is so that we do not project back onto those who suffered historical injustice our own fantasies of justice and redemption. Chattel slavery in the United States is an irredeemable fact of American history. We must confront such facts in their full horror if we are to do justice to ourselves as well as to their victims and those who descend from them, and those who "look like" they might have so descended. We must confront the true

---

4   Kat Eschner, "The horrible fate of John Casor, the first black man to be declared slave for life in America," *Smithsonian Magazine,* March 8, 2017.

nature of the legacy of slavery so that we can confront the next King. But, as the events of summer 2017 made painfully clear, a continuing inability or unwillingness to squarely confront this history contributes directly to an inability to muster the political will to exclude white supremacy and ethnic nationalism from the American public sphere.

THE HISTORICAL MISREPRESENTATION OF THE CONFEDERACY

As winter 2017 gave way to spring, the center of public controversy over the legacy of slavery and the present life of America's past in our public places shifted. The shift occurred from statements and actions by members of the Trump administration to local debates, specifically, to the debate concerning the removal of statues [5] dedicated to "Confederate heroes." These debates have centered on the removal of four statues in New Orleans commemorating Robert E. Lee, P.G.T. Beauregard, Jefferson Davis, and (most controversially [6]) the Battle of Liberty Place. This debate, I believe, must be read together with the reverberations of a similar decision to remove a statue of Robert E. Lee in Charlottesville, Virginia, the small city where I happened to be living at the time, and which was about to become far more well-known. Charlottesville's Confederate statue removal controversy probably would have gone little noticed if not for the fact that a group of white nationalists, led or at least publicly represented by the already infamous Richard Spencer, held a torchlit rally around the base of the statue [7] reminiscent of

---

5 German Lopez, "New Orleans mayor: We can't ignore the death, enslavement, and terror the Confederacy stood for," *Vox*, May 23, 2017.

6 Jamiel Lynch and Darran Simon, "P.G.T. Beauregard Confederate statue comes down in New Orleans," *CNN*, May 17, 2017.

7 Laura Vozzella, "White nationalist Richard Spencer leads torch-bearing protesters defending Lee statue," *The Washington Post*, May 14, 2017.

KKK rallies of the past. There, Spencer and his supporters loudly proclaimed statements such as "What brings us together is that we are white, we are a people, we will not be replaced," "You shall not replace us," and "Russia is our friend."

In a piece of soaring rhetoric[8] surely inspired both in tone and in content by the rhetoric of Obama (whom he quotes at a central moment in the speech), Mitch Landrieu, mayor of New Orleans, gave a serious and passionate defense of the decision to remove Confederate statues from public space that seemed to directly address the need to confront the newly emboldened white nationalism. In one of the more celebrated moments of the speech, Landrieu expressly links the continued presence of the statues to the politics of hope by sharing how a friend asked him to imagine himself as an African American mother or father whose fifth-grade daughter asks "who Robert E. Lee is and why he stands atop of our beautiful city?" Landrieu then asks himself and his listeners: "Can you do it? Can you look into that young girl's eyes and convince her that Robert E. Lee is there to encourage her? Do you think she will feel inspired and hopeful by that story? Do these monuments help her see a future with limitless potential? Have you ever thought that if her potential is limited, yours and mine are too?" The argument is clear: it is impossible for us to argue that Lee is someone who "inspires" or ought to inspire all of us, and since he cannot be someone who makes all of us "feel hopeful," each of us knows that his presence must not stand over us any longer. In Landrieu's words: "When you look into this child's eyes is the moment when the searing truth comes into focus for us. This is the moment when we know what is right and what we must do." That is, we must take the

---

8 Jack Holmes, "Read New Orleans Mayor Mitch Landrieu's remarkable speech about removing Confederate monuments," *Esquire*, May 23, 2017.

statue down. We must do so because its continuing presence in the public sphere underwrites that space as one in which some Americans cannot feel hopeful about their opportunities or even welcomed to be there.

I cannot deny that a public space that tells some of my fellow citizens that they are not welcome is not a public space in which I can feel at home. But there are norms other than the "call to feel inspired and hopeful" that operate here. And Landrieu himself acknowledges the norm, which I believe trumps the politics of home, in another, less celebrated, part of his speech, when he says: "But there are also other truths about our city that we must confront. New Orleans was America's largest slave market: a port where hundreds of thousands of souls were bought, sold, and shipped up the Mississippi River to lives of forced labor, of misery of rape, of torture." Indeed, we do need to confront those truths; this is my central point, specifically with reference to the legacy of chattel slavery in the United States. And yes, merely leaving the monuments in place, as though we can memorialize as a source of pride and identity those who stood up for slavery and against the Union, would be an utter failure to confront that history. But, it seems to me, merely removing the statues from the public space will not remove the memorial that many citizens hold in their hearts for the figures and the actions those statues symbolize.

Yes, Landrieu says that the plan is to find an appropriate place, like a museum, in which to display these monuments with context. But while Landrieu argues for the monuments to be re-situated as museum pieces,[9] for the moment at least they have simply been put in storage, where they won't contribute to our much-needed con-

---

9   Nicole Chavez and Emanuella Grinberg, "New Orleans begins controversial removal of Confederate monuments," *CNN*, April 26, 2017.

frontation with a difficult past. Landrieu's speech, taken together with the marked absence of the statues seems to me to belie his stated and laudable intention to help his fellow citizens confront "the other side" of New Orleans's history. By yoking his defense of removal to the politics of hope, Landrieu reiterates the perspective that Obama adopted in speaking to newly naturalized citizens and including slaves among those who immigrated to America. Given that many, including Frank Bruni[10] writing in *The New York Times,* cast Landrieu's speech as "just what we need to hear" in light of the resurgence of white nationalism, I am given pause. What I see in this kind of response, however laudable the intentions of the initiators of these movements, is another version of the mistake Obama made both in December 2015 on immigration.

I would humbly submit, echoing the proposal of Mayor Mike Signer of Charlottesville with respect to that city's controversial memorials to Lee and Jackson,[11] that simply removing these memorials will not do much to help us recognize today the nature of past misrecognition. Signer, whose personal views about these monuments and their legacy in their respective cities probably do not differ from Landrieu's, argued and voted against removing the Lee and Jackson monuments in Charlottesville. In an unsuccessful attempt to convince the city council not to approve the removal of the Lee statue, he suggested that it would be better to "transform in place." This proposal, an adaptation of a suggestion in the December 2016 report[12] of the "City of Charlottes-

---

10   Frank Bruni, "Mitch Landrieu reminds us that eloquence still exists," *The New York Times,* May 23, 2017.

11   Mike Signer, "Mike's statement on Charlottesville's Confederate statues," *Mike Signer,* February 6, 2017.

12   City of Charlottesville, *Blue Ribbon Commission on Race, Memorials, and Public Spaces,* December 19, 2017.

ville Blue Ribbon Commission on Race, Memorials, and Public Spaces," envisioned leaving the two statues where they are, but also building around them so as to create an open-air museum. Such a newly repopulated public space would add to the statue of Lee in Lee Park a new "memorial to civil rights victories" and, to the statue of Jackson in Jackson Park, a new "memorial to the slave auction block." With this larger cluster of memorials and explanatory plaques in the two public parks, he argued and which I also believe, we might really begin to seriously confront the issues that divide the citizens of Charlottesville and New Orleans.

This, as Signer argued, would do much more to show the full dimensions of slavery and Jim Crow in Charlottesville than merely disappearing Lee and Jackson from public view. In Signer's words: "We must see and defy these monuments to overcome what they mean. That is a more uncomfortable reality, to be sure. But I believe that this dialectical exhibit, and underlying process, of visible thesis, antithesis, and synthesis will create more vibrancy and dynamism for the progressive project in Charlottesville than the alternative."

MISREPRESENTATION, MISRECOGNITION, AND WHAT TO DO WITH THE UNFORTUNATE MEMORIALS

The Hegelian motif in Signer's statement is perhaps surprising but no accident. This is because the monuments, both in their original Jim Crow-era construction and installation, and in the debates about their removal now, have always been about the politics of recognition. Much, if not all, of our contestation in the public space is an expression of the struggle that the desire (or need) for recognition inspires, as Hegel recognized and formulated in his classic discussion of the Lord and Bondsman. I do not feel especially welcomed or honored when I walk past the monumental statue of Lee when on my way to the downtown mall or the public library in Charlottesville, and I know that many—for good reasons—feel much less welcomed and honored than I. But the point of politics is to demand that my resistance to the way those monuments interpolate and misrecognize me and my fellow citizens be recognized by my fellow citizens, including those who identify with the larger-than-life model of a Confederate general guarding over their public spaces.

I reached the judgment recorded in the previous paragraph three months before the events of August 2017. Now that they are an indelible part of recent American history, it is nearly impossible for someone who lived through 2016 and 2017 in Charlottesville, and whose views in and of American politics are like mine, to speak with anything other than utter contempt for the memorials to Confederate "heroes" and the evil they have invited into America's public places. It is just as hard to conclude anything other than that these memorials ought to be removed and destroyed at the nearest legal opportunity. But that instinct—ultimately itself an attempt to misrepresent the way the institution of slavery inextricably lives on in American politics—must be resisted. It is not easy to find the right institutional and physical settings, but there must be a way for the Jim Crow-era monuments to remain in public view, precisely as a way for us to confront the historical misrepresentations behind the "slaves were immigrants, too" rhetoric discussed above. A rhetoric that many voices, from the left as well as from the right, perpetuate.

Put another way, these monuments ought never to have been constructed, but that does not make removing them right. The detritus of history surrounds us in Charlottesville and New Orleans as elsewhere. This includes Berlin where Hegel once taught his philosophy of history, where the control center of the Nazi genocide was located, and where I write this coda to my reflections on the refusal to confront the realities of race in the United States in 2017. If the monuments concretize this for us, then let us insist on the symbolic installment of contrasting elements of our difficult past, and let us struggle together with those monuments. Let us repurpose existing monuments as we build new memorial cultures that physically embody and demonstrate the claim that the existing monuments misrepresent our shared past, as we try to discover who we have been as a people, who we are today, and who we might be tomorrow.

Michael Weinman is professor of philosophy at Bard College Berlin. He primarily works on ancient Greek thought, political philosophy, and their intersection. His most recent book The Parthenon and Liberal Education, *co-authored with Geoff Lehman, was published in the SUNY Series in Ancient Greek philosophy in March 2018.*

Andrew Boyer

What We Really Learned in Charlottesville

Finding a Way Forward

In the immediate aftermath of Heather Heyer's death and the clashing protests that led to it, Charlottesville came together as a community to show its solidarity. There were condemnations of the violence, affirmations of the statue removal, and a call for healing. Then President Donald Trump waffled on his response to the tragedy, first leaving his position ambiguous, then criticizing the white nationalists, and finally offering a disturbing comment on the moral goodness of some of the protesters who called for the violent assertion of white power. The outcry was swift and deafening; the events became a political Rorschach test during a slow August recess for Congress. Pundits and cable television and podcast broadcasters screamed themselves hoarse while journalists exacerbated their carpal tunnel, and the country bathed in the now all-too-familiar carnival of manufactured outrage, contradicting diagnoses, and forlorn grief.

By the standards of today's whiplash news cycles, the coverage was in-depth and lasting. The media did not move on from the issue so much as the media overexerted itself and then wearily stumbled on to Hurricane Harvey in Texas and Trump's DACA repeal. When the dust settled, nearly everyone agreed that white nationalists and the KKK were *morally* unacceptable. That is, representatives of various points on the political spectrum as opposed as those of Speaker

Paul Ryan[1] and Senator Kamala Harris[2] disavowed the ideology of white nationalists and white supremacists in more or less the same terms. I will return to this agreement below, but it is important to underscore that it extended only so far as condemning the *ideology behind* the "Unite the Right" rally. Many, for instance, defended the protest[3] on First Amendment grounds, arguing that the protesters followed the correct procedure and had a right to express their beliefs no matter how repugnant to the rest of society. Others decried the violence displayed by the protesters, and asserted that their race protected them[4] from the police brutality that has marked so many minority protests in recent years. Thought pieces and in-depth television segments, including on *Public Seminar,* took on all facets of the debate, from the history of the confederate statues to the rise of white nationalism. Aside from forcing statue removal into the margins of platforms for the Virginia governor's race, not much felt resolved.

Nearly eight weeks after the white nationalist demonstrations, Charlottesville is still trying to grapple with the tragedy and heal. An independent review of the weekend's events is facing increasing political pressure due to perceived ties to the city council and slow-moving pace. Economically and culturally dominated by the University of Virginia, the town is largely sympathetic to the counter-protesters and the social justice movements that were so outspoken after the infamous weekend. Professors and administrators are struggling to offer students the proper amount of emo-

---

1 Paul Ryan, "Charlottesville," *Speaker Paul Ryan,* August 21, 2017.

2 Kamala Harris, *Facebook,* August 13, 2017.

3 Logan Beirne, "Free speech under siege," *National Review,* August 29, 2017.

4 Daniel Marans, "Black leaders speak out against Charlottesville rally's 'faces of hate'," *HuffPost,* August 12, 2017.

tional security while they articulate a meaning of free speech that protects their own rights. None of these issues are new to college campuses:[5] recently cancelled speeches at Berkeley[6] are only the latest instances of a long contemporary struggle to negotiate the intersection[7] of student security and free speech ideals. The tragic developments in Charlottesville only increased the pressure on faculty to cater to their students' needs for physical security as well as to cater to their emotional needs. Faced with grievances about the violent display of hatred and bigotry, many professors do not know how to simultaneously offer the comfort that basic decency requires of them while still making a case for the free speech rights that anchor their intellectual freedom.

One of the reasons it is so hard to value free speech in the context of Charlottesville is that the protesters were not merely present to confirm their own realness to themselves and others. That is, their symbolic argument was not existential. They also provided a physical manifestation of violence promised by the ideology of the KKK and of various organizations that embrace white nationalism. Protesters marched into Lee Park armed with guns and bullet-proof vests as well as the malice[8] to use them. The decision of one protester to drive his car through a crowd of counter-protesters will be seared forever into the town's memory once the fateful stretch of road is dedicated Heather Heyer Way.

5   Mark Lilla, "How colleges are strangling liberalism," *The Chronicle of Higher Education*, August 20, 2017.

6   Taylor Lorenz, "Berkeley says 'Free Speech Week' event is canceled," *The Hill*, September 23, 2017.

7   Rachel McKinney, "The false premises of alt-right ideology," *Public Seminar*, February 20, 2017.

8   Frances Robles, "As white nationalist in Charlottesville fired, police 'never moved,'" *The New York Times*, August 25, 2017.

The violence on the ground directly correlated with the violence advocated by those groups. The protesters were there to show what it would look like to act in accordance with their beliefs. Many people, university professors or not, simply lack the will and tools to motivate people to believe in the institution of free speech when it so concretely threatens their ideas and bodies.

It is not difficult to articulate why violence is such a problem to the institution of free speech. If you take a hard line on protecting the right of people to say nearly anything they want—which in our country also means protest, fund, and organize—the assumption is that there will be more speech from other perspectives. Oliver Wendell Holmes called it the marketplace of ideas, whereas Thomas Jefferson said that "error of opinion may be tolerated where reason is left free to combat it." The language of competition and combat often gets lost when public figures rehearse these platitudes more in the model of town criers than thoughtful leaders. The violent preclusion of expression has a long history in America. There are even some journalists and academics, like Ta-Nehisi Coates at *The Atlantic*[9] and Alan Taylor here at the University of Virginia,[10] who argue that racially-motivated violence is how the United States consolidated its sovereignty during and after the Revolutionary War.[11] One major upshot of the civil rights movement was that the judicial branch of government altered or reversed nearly one hundred years of precedent regarding how the (federal) government could intervene against private citizens who used political violence.

When placed in terms of violence, it is easy to see that ideas have

---

9   Ta-Nehisi Coates, "The first white president," *The Atlantic,* October 2017.

10   Alan Taylor, *American Revolutions* (New York: W. W. Norton & Company, 2016).

11   Mindy Fullilove, Robert Fullilove, William Morrish, and Robert Sember, "Before Charlottesville there was Jamestown," *Public Seminar,* August 28, 2017.

more than consequences: they have actions attached to them. Both the protesters and counter-protesters in Charlottesville had ideas that were expressed in a number of actions spanning over a year: in the petition and city council vote [12] to remove a statue and rename a park, in the legal battle to hold a protest in the busy downtown location of the park itself, and in the occupation of the park and the surrounding blocks over the course of the weekend. Viewed retrospectively, it is easy to see this strand of actions as following from one another and in that sense necessary. But no one had to protest the city council vote, nor did they have to fight the motion to move the location of that protest. The institution of free speech, insofar as it is an institution, allowed for these actions and those which were not taken. It serves as a medium for socialization, repetition, and change by providing a shared vehicle for the transmission of ideas. So long as voting and protest do not devolve into violence, they point to the essence of free speech as an institution, namely, that it preserves *continued* action. Political, or ideological, violence prevents the abstract combativeness of words by putting *physical combat* in its place. Put simply, institutions endure, while wars end. Institutions cultivate the possibility of continuous action in which all parties participate.

The institution of free speech is not some political club to beat those with whom you do not agree; it is not a tool or a policy in the way that supporting free trade or lower taxes is. Speaking of free speech as a partisan issue undercuts its ability to preserve the very debate it subtends. More importantly, it clouds our understanding of institutions as preservers of collective action rather

---

12   Michael Weinman, "Mayoral statements on Confederate memorials: Misrepresentation and misrecognition, yet again (part two)," *Public Seminar,* June 12, 2017.

than collective ideology. I have never attended an academic debate that ended with one of the debaters admitting he was wrong and totally convinced of his opponent's argument. They always end in disagreement, and everyone knows that there will be another event next week. Academics frequently are criticized for exactly this kind of benign disagreement, but universities rely on the *institution* of free speech more than anyone else. The point of debate, insofar as it relates to the institution, is that its repeated occurrence is the organizing principle of the university. People come together and work side by side in spite of the essential difference between their ideas, because of the essential similarity of their actions. One should not push the point too far since university life is not a helpful model for politics, but there is certainly something to learn from this type of collegial, dare we say civil, association.

Take also, for example, the very exchange we enact here on *Public Seminar*. What I would like to suggest to Keval Bhatt [13] is that, no matter their intent or conviction, their pieces are not, nor will they be taken as, definitive and ultimate statements on the nature of the issues at stake in Charlottesville's statue politics. In this, I echo Michael Weinman's [14] response that it might be necessary to countenance some half-truths about the discontinuity of our mytho-poetic narrative. Isaac Ariail Reed [15] argues that we can maintain the symbolism of that narrative while leaving behind the embodiments of its fallen characters. All of this commitment to

---

13   Keval Bhatt, "Subverting the symbols of white supremacy: The wolf and the fox," *Public Seminar,* October 17, 2017.

14   Michael Weinman, "Charlottesville, Thomas Jefferson, and America's fate," *Public Seminar,* October 22, 2017.

15   Isaac Ariail Reed, "Jefferson's two bodies: Memory, protest, and democracy at the University of Virginia and beyond," *Public Seminar,* October 19, 2017.

discourse is precisely the element of our political theology that is sorely missing today. It is no half-truth that Jefferson believed in the new republic enough to suffer defeat to Adams in 1796 and run again in 1800. But when given the choice between reconciliation within the existing institutions and breaking with the institutions of the Union, *Lee and others chose to fight.* We must once more highlight the actions that enable our nation to so much as have a "public space," actions which draw us together much more than the ideas that we may discuss once we arrive in the metasocial agora.

In one of the most quoted passages from *Democracy in America,* Tocqueville calls association the mother of all sciences in the republic. While many critics today try to implicitly discredit his account of political life by highlighting the exclusionary nature of institutions[16] in early America, they miss his point. It is not that the first generations of Americans shared complete political agreement or religious and cultural unity (they shared neither). Rather, Tocqueville is drawing our attention to the way association teaches people the practice of politics, more so than the ideas of politics. These practices are the bedrock of institutions because they enable people to come together time and time again to disagree without losing the motivating principle underlying their gathering. The United States has never realized the enlightenment ideals enshrined in the Declaration of Independence. It is the promise of our institutions that allow for us to try to actualize them at all.

We need not romanticize past Congresses to decry the current state of debate in that institution. Instead of functioning as a model for the institution of free speech, with vigorous disagreement grounded in institutional pride and similar habits, our

---

16 Bhatt, "Subverting the symbols of white supremacy."

lawmakers invoke their staunch disagreements as excuses for disrupting decades old traditions like the filibuster and regular order. Roy Moore, who recently won a heated Republican primary to serve as the junior U.S. Senator from Alabama, wielded a pistol[17] at a rally and promised never to compromise on his principles. Many will be quick to point out the caning of Charles Sumner as an example of violence in Congress, but we must remind such cynics of the historical context of that event. The antebellum period was home to a much stricter code of personal honor[18] — as Trump's Chief of Staff, and retired General John Kelly, recently reminded us with respect to Lee himself.[19] As Kelly himself seemed to miss, or at least minimize, that time and Lee's personal honor were of a piece with the foment that caused the Civil War, hardly a lodestar of institutional ethics in its threat to the core of American government. It was precisely this shared sense of honor that could have kept the rebels in the Union. In this light, what Kelly calls "a failure to compromise" appears more like a failure to see the commonality among the representatives who would soon no longer be serving "on different sides of the aisle" in a single House.

After Charlottesville, it was easy to see how radical agendas manifested in behavior that was outside the bounds of acceptable civil habits. But we need to be attentive to the habits of ideology even when they do not involve violence. In many ways, the breakdown of our institutions has foretold this rise in violent political action,

---

17 Rebecca Savransky, "Roy Moore pulls out gun while speaking at rally," *The Hill*, September 26, 2017.

18 Joanne B. Freeman, *Affairs of Honor: National Politics in the New Republic* (New Haven: Yale University Press, 2002)..

19 Eli Rosenberg and Cleve R. Wootson Jr., "John Kelly calls Robert E. Lee an 'honorable man' and says 'lack of compromise' caused the Civil War," *The Washington Post*, October 31, 2017..

rather than the other way around. When our political leaders prioritize ideology at any cost, it compromises the faith that there will be another day and another *metaphorical* "fight." If violence excludes the losers absolutely, ideological foreclosure imitates this and perhaps foreshadows it, instead of giving persons stock in the shared habits of debate. That is, people start to feel that there is no point to debating at all unless they win. American political history is rife with associations, so much so that another University of Virginia historian, Brian Balogh, has argued that we are, in our essence, an associational state.[20] We must remember the importance of habitual institutions instead of stressing the ideological differences between us. Our nation, notwithstanding its long history of ideological political culture, has always sustained itself on our material and pragmatic habits. Our political debates must *recognize* these habits, and the associations and institutions that are born of these habits, as essential to our present and our past if we are to maintain some semblance of ourselves as Americans in the future.

Andrew Boyer graduated from the University of Virginia in 2017 with a B.A. in political philosophy. He was still living in Charlottesville during the course of the protests and counter-protests. He now resides in Washington, D.C., and works in the House of Representatives. Originally published in Public Seminar, *November 9, 2017.*

---

20 Brian Balogh, *The Associated State: American Government in the Twentieth Century* (Philadelphia: University of Pennsylvania Press, 2015).

Isaac Ariail Reed

Jefferson's Two Bodies

Interpretations of a Statue at the University of Virginia

I. STATUE POLITICS

Visitors to the University of Virginia, and those of us who work there, cannot miss the large statue of Thomas Jefferson at the forefront of the campus, just north of the Rotunda. This representation of Jefferson appears to look down over those working and studying at the university, which opened in 1819 under his direction.

On the night of September 12, 2017, a group of students shrouded the statue of Jefferson. They did so in memoriam of Heather Heyer, who was killed a month before by a white supremacist when she was protesting the fascist rally in downtown Charlottesville on August 12. They did so in protest of the university's paltry response to the violent fascists on its lawn—and gathering at this same statue—on the night of August 11. The shrouding of the Jefferson statue[1] was also meant to protest the university's ongoing complicity with everyday white supremacy in the United States. Jefferson was labelled a "racist and a rapist" by these students, and the message "Black Lives Matter" was combined with "Fuck White Supremacy."

It is perhaps worth noting that this action of September 12 took place one day after the local chapter of Young Americans

1   Keval Bhatt, "Subverting the symbols of white supremacy: The wolf and the fox," *Public Seminar*, October 17, 2017

for Freedom draped the statue of Homer that sits at the center of the University of Virginia lawn in the American flag, as part of a memorial event (also sponsored by the Burke Society) in honor of those who died in the terrorist attacks of September 11, 2001. This is simply to say that statue politics, and the engagement with the built environment by students, is an ongoing, complex, and multi-vocal process in the locale of the university, though the trajectories of these re-presentations of statues through the (fragmented) media system varies significantly.

The students who shrouded Jefferson inserted themselves and their message into a series of events that had been unified by their focus on statues that value and exalt the Confederacy. In particular, their actions referenced the conflict over the statues of Robert E. Lee and "Stonewall" Jackson in Charlottesville; more broadly they referenced statues in Richmond, Virginia, and statue removal in New Orleans, Louisiana. Thus, by shrouding the statue of Jefferson, these students pulled the memory of the author of the Declaration of Independence—that document so useful to Frederick Douglass, Martin Luther King Jr. and so many others—into a conversation that has most often focused on the traitors to, rather than the architects of, the American republic.

Monuments honoring the Confederacy exist throughout the United States, mostly, but not exclusively, in the south; many were built in the early part of the twentieth century to put on a pedestal those who fought in defense of slavery, and their erection was intended to legitimate the project of racial hierarchy in the Jim Crow era. This was a hierarchy enforced by repeated violence and institutionalized racial terror, and the statues of Lee and Jackson—imposing, militaristic—certainly represent *both* the violence of the Civil War and the violence of the Jim Crow era. The city of Charlottesville has *officially and semi-permanently* done to the representations of Lee and Jackson what the students did *unofficially and ephemerally* to the representation of Jefferson on campus—it has shrouded them.

The president of the University of Virginia reacted very differently to the shrouding of Jefferson by her students than she did to the shrouding of Confederate generals. In an email sent to alumni, she expressed her disdain for the students' action, insisting that in shrouding the statue the students were "desecrating ground that many of us consider sacred." She also hailed her alumni (and, presumably, her donors), generationally:

> In your own college days, many of you experienced protests and activism at UVA. The war in Vietnam, Watergate, 9/11, and many other issues have been discussed, debated, and protested at UVA. We are at another such point. I prefer the process of discussion and debate, and the debate is happening here with a wide variety of guest speakers, panels, and other opportunities to look at underlying issues. That there is also activism should not be a surprise to any of us.[2]

This email did not mention slavery; and it drew a bright line between "debate and discussion" and "activism," with the clear implication that activists were not debaters.

The email she sent to the current university community was different. To the professoriate, employees, and students, she expressed "strong disagreement" with the "protesters' decision" (thus suggesting that these students *were* part of "debate"), and dedicated a paragraph to Jefferson's ownership of slaves, the enslaved labor that built

2 Andrew Cain, "U.Va. President Teresa Sullivan: Protesters who shrouded Jefferson statue were 'desecrating' sacred ground," *Richmond Times-Dispatch*, September 13, 2017.

the first buildings of the university and served its students, and the nearly century-long period between emancipation and the integration of the University of Virginia, during which black Americans worked for, but could not enroll at, UVA.

The two emails sent—it must be said, it was a rather unstrategic move, given that both quickly appeared online at *The Washington Post*—reveal much about the cleavages in American politics. They also articulate a fundamental theoretical difficulty concerning the relationship of speech to conduct. They leave us wondering: in the eyes of the university, are the "activists" *saying something*, something that can be responded to, and if so, what are they saying? Or are they *merely* bodies in space, relatively mute? Of course, bodies in space also articulate meaning. One possibility for pursuing an answer to these questions is to theorize legally about protected speech. Herein, I pursue a strictly semiotic analysis instead. What is at stake, in the shrouding of Jefferson and the university president's reaction to it? What are the meanings— depth and surface, present/past/future, fractured and whole— that are evoked by the statue and its shrouding? While I cannot, in this short essay, adequately analyze this multiplicity, I do think we can begin to see what is at stake by articulating a theoretical language for analysis, and using that language to venture some interpretations.

II. THE PRESIDENT'S TWO BODIES AND AMERICAN POLITICAL THEOLOGY

We might begin by asking what is involved in the veneration of presidents—university presidents (such as Sullivan, and Jefferson) and founders (such as Jefferson), but also American presidents (including, but not limited to, those who are revered as "founders" of the United States). The American executive branch has a special history, owing to the way it emerged as part of the answer, within a republic, to the idea of sovereignty in a monarchy. Sovereignty, in this latter sense, was grounded in the legal fiction and cultural schema known as the "king's two bodies." In this schema, a series of representations and legal arguments indicated that the king's "second body" was unchanging (unlike a given king's mortal "first body"), and, as such, contained within it the body politic, whose existence could continue indefinitely into the future. As Ernst Kantorowicz showed in great detail,[3] this cultural and legal schema was immensely productive as a framework for imagining power. For the king's two bodies allowed one to imagine and justify the conduct of state actions in perpetuity and with regularity. For example, under the auspices of the king's second body, one could tax yearly in the name of "King and Crown" (It also, Kantorowicz shows, structures Shakespeare's *Richard II*). And so, the idea of the king's two bodies is the cultural-and-legal dimension of the absolutist origins of the modern state.

The American republic and the revolution that led to it disrupted and replaced this foundational legal fiction. Indeed, all three of the eighteenth-century Atlantic revolutions contributed to the destruction of the idea that "the king is dead, long live the king" can serve as the ongoing legal and cultural basis for peace, prosperity, and political and social order. However, as an element of culture, the king's two bodies did not disappear. Rather, it made its way into post-monarchic politics in complicated and sometimes counterintuitive ways. The king's two bodies lived on *not only* in the Constitution's official granting of rather extensive powers to

---

3   Ernst H. Kantorowicz, *The King's Two Bodies: A Study in Medieval Political Theology* (Princeton: Princeton University Press, 2016).

the presidency (which scholars have long noted, pace Hamilton's "protesting too much" to the contrary in *Federalist 67* and *69–70*, as a kind of British-facing replacement of king-in-parliament with president-and-congress—for the latest version of this argument see Eric Nelson's *The Royalist Revolution* [4]), *but also* in the social interpretation of presidents themselves.

Indeed, starting with George Washington, many of the presidents of the republic became, even while alive, mythical. Whoever occupies the office is, in the interpretation of their lives, fortunes, and loves, a central location of American political theology. That presidents have two bodies—in cultural life if not in the law—is what explains the obsession, throughout the long history of the republic, with the bodies of presidents and their relationship to the social or political "body" of the country (for instance, it suggests a ground for the otherwise incomprehensible fascination and ongoing discussion of the size of the hands of the current office holder). For, if there is one location where the symbols of American democracy are the most charged, the most overwrought, the most wildly undisciplined, the most intense, it is in the semiosis that flows through the flesh and blood of the chief executive (the first body as representation of the second), and thus through the iconic representations of that first body as well. Via this schema, the president's mind, house, family, accoutrements, ideas, writings, jokes, preferences in sexual activities, preferences in cigars, and exercise habits are given a double significance. They are subjected, via writing and art, to a kind of perpetual motion machine, a seemingly infinite source of semiotic energy. In the presidency, the framework of the king's two bodies meets its

---

4   Eric Nelson, *The Royalist Revolution: Monarchy and the American Founding* (Cambridge: Harvard University Press, 2017).

replacement in the form of the idea of the *people* as sovereign, and at this particular location in public culture, other meetings between the pre- and post-revolutionary worlds also take place: charismatic and authoritarian leadership meet the idea of a public servant, and the very possibility of government by the many meets the inspiring twice-told tale of the individual leader who founds, saves, or remakes the republic.

Certainly, the representation of Jefferson was, and continues to this day to be, one such generator of semiotic energy. But the president's two bodies is not a matter confined to the reverence directed at the founders of the republic. The political scientist Michael Rogin showed quite clearly[5] the importance of this scheme for comprehending the rhetoric emanating from, and swirling around, Abraham Lincoln, Woodrow Wilson, Richard Nixon, and Ronald Reagan; sociologist Jeffrey C. Alexander used the concept[6] to analyze the campaigns of Barack Obama and John McCain. Rogin explains the utility of using the king's two bodies to analyze the two bodies of various presidents this way:

> The doctrine of the king's two bodies offers us a language in which confusions between person, power, office, and state become accessible. It alerts us to how certain chief executives found problematic their bodies mortal and the human families and dwelling places that housed them; how they sought transcendent authority and immortal identity in the White House, absorbing the body politic in themselves; how they committed massive violence against the political institutions of the fathers and the lives of the republic's sons; and how

5 Michael Rogin, *Ronald Reagan The Movie: And Other Episodes in Political Demonology* (Oakland: University of California Press, 1988).

6 Jeffrey C. Alexander, *The Performance of Politics: Obama's Victory and the Democratic Struggle for Power* (Oxford: Oxford University Press, 2010).

their own presidential death consummated or shattered their project.[7]

The recurrence of contests of interpretation about the president's two bodies can also provide insight into the current moment. It helps us comprehend how a large percentage of the American population could not accept, at a "gut" level, that Obama was not only an elected leader but a culturally legitimate sovereign, as Eric Michael Dyson has studied.[8] Indeed, some such persons sit in Congress. The *basic* explanation for this is racism, fear of the other, the scare politics that politicians used to connect American blacks to "foreign" Muslims, etc. But the basic explanation is not enough; there is more.

The disgust that Obama generated as an executive extended beyond the ongoing life of everyday American racism and xenophobia. Something further was afoot, as evidenced by the tremendous popularity of the controversy—stoked by Donald Trump—over Obama's birth certificate. I would hypothesize that the rejection of Obama was an interpretation not simply about his actual body, and not only about his "identity," but about his *ability to grow a second body, and thus contain within himself the body politic.* Certain skin colors, in American politics, have long signified certain meanings and invited certain contestations, and nothing is perhaps more contested, and more likely to produce violent reaction, than an enhancement—or perceived enhancement—of black power. But even beyond this, Obama's skin color signified for some parts of the electorate an unallowable profanation of the

---

7   Rogin, *Ronald Reagan*, p. 82.

8   N. D. B. Connolly, "'The black presidency: Barack Obama and the politics of race in America,' by Michael Eric Dyson," *The New York Times*, February 2, 2016.

sacred second body of the president, which, in a republic, is taken to represent "the people."

If we understand American politics as, in part, constituted via the political semiosis that relates the second body of the president to the first, we can begin to see what is at stake here. If American politics is, in part, *political theology,* the president's second body works as follows: the signifier of the president (his actual body, or iconic representations of that body) somewhat mystically represents the people, the state, and the "idea of America" all at once. And these are all extraordinarily contested notions. Beyond and behind such contestation, however, lies violence. In particular, many of the interpretations made in reaction to the "occupation" of the White House by a black man have advocated violence. "Charlottesville," was, in part, the result of this cultural maelstrom.

Ta-Nehisi Coates's argument that Trump is the "first white president"[9] of the United States illuminates this point. Trump's whiteness is not merely everyday whiteness, but rather that of a *recovery of a white political body that excludes the nonwhite as profane.* We can add to Coates's analysis an understanding of Trump's campaign magic in the mystical terms of the king's two bodies. Trump appeared, to his base, not as a buffoon, but as the kind of person who could make the profane sacred again. It was a strange loop: Trump broke every rule for access to the presidency that Obama, in his personal conservatism and careful rhetoric, followed closely. Most importantly, Trump's spiral of charismatic success[10] appeared to depend on what would have been, for a "normal" candidate, a series of campaign-ending scandals: the

9   Ta-Nehisi Coates, "The first white president," *The Atlantic,* October 2017.

10   Isaac Ariail Reed, "Trump as Ubu Roi: On the charismatic appeal of vulgarity," *Public Seminar,* June 6, 2017.

naked pictures of his foreign-born wife on the front page of the newspaper, his recorded discussions of sexual assault, and his spoken profanity. Beneath all of this was a proposition that Trump offered his audiences, which Coates has grasped and analyzed with great clarity. Trump's message was: everything is fallen in this corrupt world of a black presidency, so why not make the profane the new sovereign? We know from Georges Bataille [11] (and, unfortunately, from Joseph Goebbels) that that which is profane can be made, via the mobius strip of desire, into the sacred.

III. JEFFERSON'S SECOND BODY AND EVERYDAY LIFE AT THE UNIVERSITY OF VIRGINIA

Jefferson's second body is, in American national culture, a location for plenty of debate. Some of this debate touches on the founders generally—given that the wealth and power of Virginia was central to the creation of the republic, Jefferson is but one of several mythologized figures who not only owned slaves, but wrote the Constitution and defended it in such a way that they could continue the practice. Jefferson's legacy is profoundly paradoxical; if negotiated carefully, this paradox could serve an explicitly progressive and even civic purpose. For, at the national level, the meeting point of memory and historical scholarship is a space where critique can enter public life. Citizens can be asked— as they are often asked, on the slavery tour at Monticello—to think about the contradictions between Jefferson's ideals and his daily life, and in particular about how such memories could be used to build a more perfect union.

---

11 Georges Bataille, *The Accursed Share: Volumes II and III* (Cambridge: The MIT Press, 1992).

And then there is the Declaration. The radicalism of the Declaration of Independence is undeniable—for its own time,[12] the twentieth century,[13] and the twenty-first.[14] The continued, contested interpretation of this text, whose primary author was also the master of Monticello, seems worthwhile indeed. It is, furthermore, the University of Virginia itself that has an unparalleled scholarly tradition for thinking about Jefferson and the early American republic, for investigating the contradictions in his writings and his life, and for considering his contributions to political philosophy. I suspect many of those who share the progressive ambitions of Danielle Allen's book *Our Declaration*,[15] and appreciate this scholarly tradition, were likely to cringe at the students' shrouding of Jefferson, for the simple reason that it would appear that the left may be giving up one of its most important symbolic resources.

Eager to own up to the sins of the man, many progressives nonetheless wish to embrace the meanings of the text of the Declaration; from afar, it may have appeared that the students were, in a sense, buying into what one might speculate would be Richard Spencer's own interpretation of Jefferson (i.e., that he is "of a piece" with Jackson and Lee)—but inverting its moral evaluation (i.e., both Jefferson and the Confederate generals deserve shrouding and removal, not public commemoration and valorization). But

---

12 Clifford Geertz, *Local Knowledge: Further Essays in Interpretive Anthropology* (New York: Basic Books, 2008).

13 Jacques Derrida, "The declaration of independence," *New Political Science* 15 (1986): 7-16.

14 Danielle Allen, *Our Declaration: A Reading of the Declaration of Independence in Defense of Equality* (New York: W. W. Norton & Company, 2014).

15 Gordon S. Wood, "A different idea of our declaration," *The New York Review of Books*, August 14, 2014.

matters—especially in the iconic world where aesthetics meets morality and politics—are not so straightforward. For one must recognize, perhaps, that the very eagerness of the progressive left to own up to the sins of the man is, in a sense, captured by a politics of splitting and disavowal; by manifesting the kind of depths of darkness implied by the shroud, there is something in this act that calls for further reflection.

Furthermore, meanings are also local.[16] The national and international debates about Jefferson and the importance of his memory to the continuation of the republic and the creation of a "more perfect union" intersect and shape, but do not exhaust or entirely determine the meanings of Jefferson that are made and remade at the University of Virginia every day. And it was, in part, that everyday context that helps us interpret the shrouding of Jefferson. Locally, there is in everyday life here a *banal sacralization of Jefferson's second body* that is unthinking and personalistic. It glorifies, implicitly and explicitly, Jefferson the man qua patriarch and head of household. Here again, we find Kantorowicz calling us back to the king's two bodies. For Kantorowicz, the representation of kings that appeared on various objects, including those used daily, like coins, inscribed into everyday life a kind of identification of king and public—in an absolutist state that is centered on a monarch, the king is the only truly public person. In the public, everyday life of the University of Virginia and its environs, something similar happens with Jefferson's second body; this meaning circulates to the point of saturation, but it is quite distinct from the national memory contests over founding fathers with which we are all, in the United States, familiar. In this strictly local banal sacralization, it is not our historians' careful scholarship on Jefferson that choreographs campus. Rather, on "grounds" (the name itself is a kind

16 Geertz, *Local Knowledge.*

of sacralization), the student, the employee, and the administrator are invited to experience Jefferson as a saintly presence. We find, in myriad little signifiers, a public interpretation of Jefferson's fatherly wisdom.

This interpretation—of Jefferson as a saintly and wise father—inhabits our classrooms, our coffee shops on campus (there is even a chalk portrait of Jefferson in the Starbucks in Nau Hall), and every nook and cranny of our buildings. The casual references to his having "built" the university (when in fact it was built by enslaved persons); the habitual reaching for his wisdom, insight, sayings, and words on seemingly every occasion of professional significance; the ongoing connection to his literal home at Monticello, presented repeatedly as glorious; all of these serve to instantiate a certain fantasy that has little to do with the subtlety and contradictions of Jefferson's life and thought, or the difficult and contentious history of the American republic. Rather, the day-to-day fantasy presented at the university goes something like this: "Jefferson's sacred genius legitimated his power, and that genius was the genius of the father of a household, who built the future so his young charges could live and work freely on their studies."

This is an emotionally appealing idea, but it is precisely the problem. For what, exactly, is the household we are imagining here? If all of these icons of the first body of Jefferson produce, in this locale, a kind of look-and-feel through which a sacred second body of Jefferson is instantiated, we perhaps should ask directly, "What does the University of Virginia look and feel like?" One answer to this question is quite well known: it refers to Jefferson's own distinctly classical[17] preferences in architec-

17   Krishan Kumar, "Mr Jefferson's university," *The Times Literary Supplement*, September 19, 2017.

ture. But the problem with this interpretation is that there is a chain of signification that begins in the experience of "grounds," but does not end in Athens. For, the one place in the world that looks the most like the University of Virginia is . . . Monticello. Monticello was and is a lot of things; but more than anything else, it was a plantation. The banal reverence invited by the statue of Jefferson, and by the representation of him that inhabits the campus, encodes this meaning.

To be clear, this is not the only meaning to be made out of Jefferson's statue. *However,* there are limits to interpretation, and certain interpretations have an inner logic that it is radically disingenuous to deny (this, after all, is the point of semiotics as an analytical standpoint: culture does not come in small pieces, it comes in complexes of signs and meanings). *If* the university is repeatedly interpreted via the metaphor of the *household,* and *if* Jefferson's statue is interpreted as referring to the sacred Jefferson as the *head of household,* then an unavoidable conclusion of this interpretation is that the sovereignty of the house accrues to the father, and that in Jefferson's life and times, that was a violent sovereignty of white over black. I believe that many progressives, liberals, and conservatives in the United States would agree that this specific meaning of "Jefferson" is one that should be directly negated. So why do we tolerate it and promulgate it, instead? This, at least, was the uncomfortable question that the shrouding caused me to ask myself.

The shrouding of Jefferson by the students may have been *unstrategic* vis-à-vis the pursuit of concrete progressive goals. I do not think it made life easier for the coalitional left, on campus or, insofar as pictures of the shrouding were taken up nationally, in the United States. But politics is not reducible to concrete goals; it is not only a means-ends game. It is also a struggle over worldview and ethos. This was made clear by the defensive and rearguard reaction of the president of the University of Virginia—and others around campus—to her students. The students' brief and ephemeral negating of the representation of Jefferson elicited moral condemnation. This condemnation revealed the persistence of meanings-as-everyday-feelings that many of us would rather ignore. Note: the students did not vandalize the statue; the shroud was cut down; the statue stands exactly as it was before. What they conducted, then, was not a *desecration*. In so far as it felt like one, we need think through carefully what, exactly, is so discomfiting about this. After all, "rapist" is a charged word, but there is no living person who, on the basis of the students' actions, is *actually being charged* with this crime in our legal system. As for "racist," well, what other term is more appropriate for white persons who owned black slaves? Surely the slogans attached to Jefferson's statue had more *historical accuracy* as signs-pointing-to-referents than did the draping of the statue of Homer in the American flag? So, what, then, is the problem with this "activism?" Why is it so "radical"?

IV. CRITIQUE OF THE DEFENSE OF JEFFERSON
The continued presence of the specific statue of Jefferson referenced in this article is not, in and of itself, inherently ideological; many reconfigurations of both the built environment around the statue, and of our own behaviors vis-à-vis the representations of Jefferson on campus, are possible. For example, shortly after the shrouding, an artist's reinterpretation of the very idea of "putting someone on a pedestal" was installed in front of the statue—to quite interesting effect. So, variability in interpretation obtains.

However, claims—by the university president and others—that this act by students was a *desecration* are dissimulation loaded down with ideology. What, really, is this "ground that many of us consider sacred?" I suspect that there is more than one sacred thing about Jefferson, and I also suspect that what I find profane about Jefferson, others (such as Richard Spencer) find attractive, even sacred. This is to say that interpretations of Jefferson are not sealed off from conduct; they carry with them suggestions and imperatives, tendencies to bend action in one direction rather than another, and articulations of the present with the future and the past.

To call what the students did a desecration, as the president did in her email, lacked normative validity, but sociologically it was rather predictable. The president of the University of Virginia, whose very office "descends" from Jefferson, fell into the allure of the "president's two bodies"—in both senses, local and national—at exactly the wrong moment. Her words coded her own students as profane and uncivil, as engaged in activism without speech, despite their peaceful conduct, despite their clearly articulated demands, and despite their specifically non-permanent resignification of the statue. Most importantly, the president coded the students as uncivil, *despite the recent storming of campus by white supremacists whose advocacy of, and practice of, violence against nonwhites is on display for all to see.* This was, then, the specifically cultural failure of the administration, and it is one that continues on campus.

While President Sullivan attempted, again, to elevate Jefferson himself as the paragon of civil disagreement—implying, as her emails so often do, that he is the signified to which all good signifiers in the USA can eventually be traced—the students who shrouded the statue performed precisely the inverse of this politically naïve, if sociologically predictable, "defense" of "sacred ground." By compelling those who saw pictures of the shrouding to confront Jefferson's biography, they sought, not to erase the history of Jefferson as "founder" of the United States and the university, but rather to *debunk the myth of Jefferson's second body as the pristine, sacred, and mystical inhabitant of the bricks and mortar of the university.* What they attacked, then, was the norm that something about Jefferson's life and times can and should choreograph our actions and interactions on a daily basis at the University of Virginia. And in doing so, they participated in a long tradition of debunking-as-democratic-action. They engaged in conduct that demanded reinterpretation and the reflexive examination of one's everyday feel for the life of the university, and they demanded a reconfiguration of conduct by the administration, given the exigencies of the political moment. It remains to be seen whether the university community, and the administration in particular, will meet this challenge.

In solidarity with the students, then, I can say the following: in the lifeworld of the University of Virginia today, we have a taller order than that of simply recognizing and mentioning the contradictions of Jefferson's life and times. *Because of the manifest authoritarianism on the rise in the democracies of the West, because of the violence perpetrated in Charlottesville and directed at our students, and because the United States must recognize its multiethnic composition and abandon the dominance of any racial group if it is to survive as a democracy in the twenty-first century,* [18] *we must grasp how the banal veneration of Jefferson's sacred second body invites the performance and experience of whiteness as power.*

This recognition will not, in my view, require us to take down the statue. But it does require us to give up on the easy

---

18   Danielle Allen, "Charlottesville is not the continuation of an old fight. It is something new," *The Washington Post,* August 13, 2017.

veneration of Jefferson as the daily substrate of our noble purpose as scholars and researchers. We cannot both (1) revere our university's founder in the particular role of patriarch, and (2) move forward together as a group in equal dialogue across difference. If we are committed to open and free inquiry, argument and disagreement without violence, and the building of a society in which all have access to the sacred rights of individuals that Jefferson himself wrote about so eloquently—rights that are so unequally distributed in the United States today—we must be willing to let go of Jefferson's sacred second body as the animating ghost of our classrooms. We must, instead, understand the founder of the University of Virginia as an author and politician to confront and discuss. And this means less deference, more activity, and, in particular, the discovery of new models of democratic action. On this front, our students have themselves provided a model. Perhaps we should consider their "activism," then, indeed, *democratic communication.*

V. OF ICONS AND GOLEMS

I have, at certain moments in this semiotic analysis, referred to both the statue of Jefferson, and other representations of his visage on campus, as iconic. This is useful for understanding the link between signs and experience, because the phenomenon of iconicity suggests a link between semiotics and hermeneutics. In an essay on icons and power,[19] Jeffrey C. Alexander writes that "everyday experience is iconic, which means that self, reason, morality, and society are continually defined in aesthetic, deeply experiential ways." In reviewing Immanuel Kant's notorious

19   Jeffrey C. Alexander, "Iconic consciousness: The material feeling of meaning,"
Thesis Eleven 103, no. 1 (2010): 10–25.

racism as part of his essay, Alexander notes the "normative risk" in analyzing "aesthetic surface and moral depth." He is referring to the way in which, in providing an interpretation of others' interpretations of experience, one is entering into the fray of *ought* with one's analysis of *is*.

The students who shrouded Jefferson put the iconic experience of "grounds" up for analysis. Their actions demanded a reflexive consideration of the aesthetic-moral-political experience of the built environment at the University of Virginia. And indeed, many elite universities have found themselves in the middle of similar protests about their buildings. We should not, as intellectuals, dismiss this—as so many cynical critics would— as "merely symbolic" politics. Rather, these protests should be seen as interrogations of the invited experience and interpretation encoded into the material environment of some of the most iconic places of the United States. Especially when, as is the University of Virginia, a university is public—a place where state meets society—this experience takes on special meanings. The experience of these built environments is held out to the entire American population as an ideal for which to strive. Advertisements during the broadcast of college football games, seen by millions, ask plaintively: what could be more wonderful than to be a student in the great halls of an elite American university? The students who shrouded Jefferson have put those of us who were *once students at these places* on notice. We must carefully interpret and explain *what makes certain signs overflow with meaning, generate passionate emotion, and occupy an outsized place in the consciousness of persons.* For, when signs do this, they evoke by their very presence a choreography of conduct.

To ask about sticky signs at the university is to ask openly the taboo question forced upon us by the moment, one which can no longer be held at arm's length: why is the architecture of the University of Virginia so attractive to fascists, white supremacists, and neo-Nazis in the first place? One of the students who shrouded the statue of Jefferson held up a sign that itself performed a mimesis: "Hate has had a place here for 200 years," the sign read, with the numerals "200" written in direct imitation of the logo the university chose to brand is bicentennial. This is what we might call iconic politics.

But again, meanings are local, and they are always, perhaps, even stranger than they first appear. At its bicentennial celebrations, the University of Virginia hired a professional Jefferson impersonator. The website for said professional describes him as the exact height, weight, and "general appearance" of Jefferson. A surface interpretation would explain this is relatively inconsequential, if perhaps misguided, fun. After all, it is not as if the returning alumni and big donors were actually going to be convinced that Jefferson himself was walking the campus ("grounds"). But a more speculative interpretation of this publicity stunt would wonder if it means that the statue on a pedestal in front of the University of Virginia is not only an icon, but also a golem. This is a disturbing possibility. In the classic narratives, golems often escape the control of those who raise them, wreaking havoc on the very communities they are supposed to protect (we might say: liberals who wish to raise the "liberal Jefferson," beware of what you are raising—that Virginia clay has more than the liberal Jefferson within it). But we must also ask: is it possible that the psychic need for a living Jefferson on campus might reflect a *mystic* interpretation of the American past, which manifests in consciousness as a certain attraction to nation, race, and order? The golem of Prague was raised to protect a minority community from the violent pogroms of a wicked and prejudiced majority. When I lie awake at night, I fear that the golem of Charlottesville might be the symbolic entryway for the precise opposite in American society today. Let us stop raising him from the earth before it is too late.

ACKNOWLEDGMENTS

The author thanks Jennifer Bair, Michael Weinman, Abigail Moore, Fiona Greenland, and Pilar Plater for reading, comments, and suggestions. He also thanks the students in his Sociology of Power and Authority class in the Fall of 2017 at the University of Virginia for engaging in robust and enlightening discussion and debate.

Isaac Ariail Reed is associate professor of sociology at the University of Virginia. He is the author of Interpretation and Social Knowledge: On the use of theory in the human sciences and "Chains of Power and Their Representation" (Sociological Theory), and the editor, with Monika Krause and Claudio Benzecry, of Social Theory Now. Originally published on Public Seminar, October 19, 2017.

Gordon Mantler

Is it Time for the Kneeling Freedman Statue to Go?

Remolding our Political Aesthetics

At the beginning of each semester, I take my first-year college writing students at the George Washington University to Lincoln Park in the Capitol Hill neighborhood of Washington, D.C. The neighborhood park, often full of children, nannies, and dog walkers, is a perfect place for a field trip to discuss the class theme: how memorials and museums narrate U.S. history. There are two statues in Lincoln Park that I make sure we analyze: the Emancipation, or Freedman's, Memorial, built in 1876, and the Mary McLeod Bethune Memorial, erected in 1974.

The contrast between the two is striking and one reason why I take students there. The Emancipation Memorial, designed by Thomas Ball, portrays a stern Abraham Lincoln standing over a kneeling, newly-freed black man. In one of Lincoln's hands is the Emancipation Proclamation; the other floats above the prone figure's head. Based upon Archer Alexander, the last known person captured under the callous Fugitive Slave Act of the 1850s, the kneeling figure is barely clothed and has a vacant look in his eyes. A broken chain lies nearby, as does a whip. Across the park's small plaza sits a more modern memorial of Bethune, the black educator, civil rights activist, and member of President Franklin Roosevelt's "Black Cabinet." Designed by Robert Berks, best known for the bust of J.F.K. at the Kennedy Center for the Performing Arts and the Albert Einstein statue at the National Academy of

Sciences, the statue depicts a hopeful Bethune gazing upward while two children look on. She, too, holds a scroll, a symbol of her legacy being passed on to a new generation.

While I always found the Emancipation Memorial disturbing in its paternalistic Lincoln and degraded freedman, the conversation that it seems to have with the Bethune memorial makes for an instructive space about shifting values, aesthetics, and politics over time. And yet, in the wake of the Charlottesville tragedy and a rising consensus over the inappropriateness of Confederate and other offensive statues in the public square, it may well be time to retire this memorial. Even one that includes Lincoln.

As scholars and activists have pointed out, the memorial was controversial from the start. Frederick Douglass, who spoke at the dedication, decried the statue for portraying "the Negro on his knees." Unlike the current use of kneeling as solemn protest, this statue suggests that African Americans had no say in their own emancipation. This contrasts with the active role historians know African Americans played in freeing themselves—through operating the Underground Railroad, fleeing behind Union Army lines, taking up arms against the Confederacy, and any number of smaller actions. Moreover, the statue's freedman seems lost, unsure of his new freedom. Perhaps that spoke for some, but for most, freedom was a welcomed change—a change that, by the time the statue was unveiled, was at great risk under the specter of white violence and federal capitulation.

The Emancipation Memorial has endured to this point for several reasons. First because it honors the still beloved and respected 16th president, the so-called Great Emancipator and savior of the Union. Lincoln did play an important role in emancipation, albeit a more ambiguous one than is sometimes recognized. Second,

The Emancipation, or Freedman's, Memorial, built in 1876. Lincoln Park, Washington D.C. Photo © Gordon Mantler.

The Mary McLeod Bethune Memorial, erected in 1974 Lincoln Park, Washington D.C. Photo © Gordon Mantler.

and despite the ambiguous final product, the statue is one of the few primarily funded by emancipated slaves. While these funders were shut out of the design process, the statue still remains a point of pride to some African Americans. Thirdly, the memorial remains a powerful artifact of the end of Reconstruction, including Lincoln's own discomfort with black equality. Sadly, and perhaps most importantly, it is the resilience of white supremacy, on display in Charlottesville and elsewhere, which has allowed the statue to survive.

Those reasons, however, may not be enough anymore. Lincoln, of course, has his own larger-than-life memorial on the National Mall—a monument initially to saving the Union but one equally symbolic, thanks to its role in the 1963 March on Washington and other civil rights rallies, of the long black freedom struggle. Other monuments in the city, including the African American Civil War and Dr. Martin Luther King Jr. memorials—not to mention the new National Museum of African American History and Culture—better capture the agency black historical actors had. African American donors played a significant role in funding all three. And then there is the presence of the Bethune statue, built at the height of the black power movement. As my students observed, several multiracial groups of children swarmed the two playgrounds beside Bethune's memorial—an appropriate extension of her lifelong work in education. But for many of the children playing, they first had to walk by the kneeling slave. What an odd, perhaps confusing image for them to encounter on the way to play.

While I may miss the teaching moment the Emancipation Memorial offers now, were it to be removed an equally instructive lesson will take its place. The National Park Service, which maintains the space, should remove the statue—probably with the input of the surrounding neighborhood—and rededicate the park. Bethune Park, after all, has a nice ring to it.

Gordon Mantler teaches writing and history at the George Washington University. Originally published in Public Seminar, *October 17, 2017.*

Laura Goldblatt

Your Safety Is My Foremost Concern

Lessons from Charlottesville on Vulnerability and Protection

The 2017 "Summer of Hate" that culminated in Charlottesville on August 11 and 12 served as a reminder (especially to many of us working within higher education) that racism's violence, though somewhat different in its routines, has not been mitigated since the civil rights movement.

Indeed, the very form of that violence calls into question many commonsense notions of safety, particularly as our protection as citizens intersects with institutions such as the police, higher education, and domesticity. The increasing proliferation of home security systems in the United States and the call by Charlottesville's city and university officials to keep clear of the "Unite the Right" march on August 12 suggests that safety is commonly defined as the ability to shield oneself in increasingly militarized ways—either behind locked doors or in various bucolic realms—from that which threatens us.

This idea of personal safety has a corollary in the ways that institutions, and for the purpose of this piece, the University of Virginia, have sought to securitize their financial investments and the groups they purportedly serve. But the weekend of August 12 showed us in terrifying clarity that this atomized version of safety only imperils us further. By looking briefly at the ways that events unfolded at the University of Virginia and in Charlottes-ville, I intend to show that coming together, rather than retreat-ing behind locked doors, is what actually keeps communities safe.

I. THE UNIVERSITY OF VIRGINIA

On August 4, University of Virginia President Teresa Sullivan sent an email to all members of the university community encouraging them to stay away from the "Unite the Right" rally scheduled to take place one week later in downtown Charlottesville, just over a mile from the University of Virginia campus (or "grounds" as students, faculty, staff, and residents have traditionally called it). Citing the "credible risk of violence," Sullivan noted that "your safety remains my foremost concern" and argued that attending the rally, even as a counter-protester, would only "satisfy [the alt-right activists'] craving for spectacle."

Instead, she encouraged the University of Virginia community to participate in a slew of events organized by UVA faculty and staff on grounds on August 12, including discussions on constitu-tional rights, a soccer game, and a sports-themed movie night. In contrast to the threatening tableau looming just beyond grounds, Sullivan offered two hallmark comforts of the residential univer-sity: debate and recreation.

In addition to the palliative effects of Sullivan's offerings, her email message bears noting for several reasons. First, as an edict addressed only to those with a Virginia.edu email, Sullivan drew a tight circle around the groups whose safety were her primary concern. That community did not include the hundreds of service workers employed by independent contractors who labor every day to provide meals, janitorial services, and grounds keeping: tasks essential to the University of Virginia's daily operations.

Though ostensibly a public event, it is unclear how those Charlottesville residents not attached to the university would hear about the planned events and Sullivan did not suggest that the events were open to the public in her message.

Further, Sullivan's version of "community" did not include the many Charlottesville residents who find themselves priced out of neighborhoods surrounding the university, as luxury student housing complexes raise property taxes and rental rates. This was, in other words, a community defined by exclusivity rather than inclusivity, and one only available in perpetuity for a select few such as tenured faculty members or highly compensated administrators.[1] The remaining members of this community would eventually graduate out of it, or worse, find themselves on the wrong end of budget cuts and hiring freezes.

Second, Sullivan couches the workings of the University of Virginia as a safe haven, at least for those with access to its resources. But this vision of institutional harbor ignores the various ways that universities in general, and the University of Virginia in particular, imperil their surrounding communities as well as those within the university itself.

Most obviously, the "Unite the Right" rally that ended with the death of Heather Heyer was organized by two University of Virginia graduates: Richard Spencer and Jason Kessler. That the banal workings of the university—sports games and academic debate—were a part of the radicalization of two men who cite a particularly erudite (but no less horrifying) tradition of white supremacy, which claims Thomas Jefferson as one of its animating forces, was entirely elided in Sullivan's missive.

---

1   According to the University of Virginia website, UVA employs approximately 16,000 faculty and staff, not including the health system. In contrast, nearly 100,000 people live in Albemarle County.

Instead, Sullivan describes the world beyond the University of Virginia campus as vaguely threatening due to the ways that it differs from the grounds. If life within the university is defined by lecture, discovery, debate, and recreation, then the world outside it is rife with violent spectacle. Indeed, this vision of the University of Virginia follows a longstanding pattern of "protecting" the institution from external forces both through the proliferation of campus police and the incorporation of local police forces onto the campus. Though ostensibly present to protect students, especially female students from the threat of campus rape, the presence of armed police and guards on and adjacent to the university has instead resulted in the brutalization of black students, as I have analyzed with Lenora Hanson and Bennett Carpenter elsewhere.[2] While this version of academic community ignores the routinized violence that occurs on the grounds every year—from racist and anti-Semitic graffiti to hate crimes against students of color—it also casts the University of Virginia as a safe haven only for those already protected by its various institutional privileges.

And yet, this version of safety, of putting up barriers to entry and retreating into routine, proved ineffective. Not only did white supremacist groups (predictably) march on campus wielding torches that they used to beat students surrounding Thomas Jefferson's statue on the north side of the Rotunda on August 11, the events planned for the University of Virginia were all canceled on August 12 after the governor of Virginia declared a state of emergency.

---

2   Bennett Carpenter, Laura Goldblatt, & Lenora Hanson, "The university must be defended! Safe spaces, campus policing and university-driven gentrification," In/Security. *Special issue of English Language Notes* 54, no. 2 (2016): 191–198.

Still, this ineffectiveness pales beside the risk that the university's version of safety posed to the Charlottesville community as a whole. As I will show later, in casting itself as a shield against certain kinds of violence (and certain kinds of people), the University of Virginia merely redirected that violence against communities already vulnerable to it.

II. PUBLIC SAFETY ON AUGUST 12

Despite its violent and tragic end, the events of August 12 provide a different view of safety, one that suggests that joining together to protect the vulnerable is a more efficacious method, and a model to follow moving forward.

In this volume and elsewhere, many others have documented and written about the violent eruptions that defined August 12, from the parking lot beating of DeAndre Harris while police stood down and watched, to the shots fired on Market Street, to Heyer's murder. What has received less careful attention is the violence that was avoided due to community defense.

In the days leading up to the rally, Brandon Collins, the full-time organizer for the Charlottesville Public Housing Association of Residents had asked the Charlottesville Police Department to block off street parking in the areas adjacent to public and low-income housing complexes in downtown Charlottesville. As evidence, he cited online threats against public housing made by prospective attendees of the "Unite the Right" rally, as well as recent precedent.

After members of the Ku Klux Klan were escorted from the park where they held their rally on July 8 in Charlottesville, those attendees drove around and through public housing complexes in the area, strewing trash and shouting slurs at residents. Collins noted that the "Unite the Right" rally posed a unique threat to these communities: the organizers of the rally could, after all, read maps and, given the extensive planning that had gone into the event and its aftermath, might very well have plans to once again terrorize poor communities of color in the area. Collins reasoned that while parking prohibitions could not forestall the entirety of the threat, such regulations would at the very least provide a buffer between alt-right activists and extremely low-income residents of Charlottesville. Collins's request was denied.

Soon after the governor declared a state of emergency and officially shut down the "Unite the Right" rally, anti-racist protesters heard that a group of alt-right activists were on the march to a low-income housing complex to menace—and perhaps maim—residents. The anti-racists organized quickly, and began marching towards Friendship Court, the threatened complex. They arrived to find a group of sympathizers who explained that they had heard the call earlier, banded together, and successfully expelled those wishing to do harm to the community. While one group stayed behind to keep watch over Friendship Court, another marched back towards the downtown mall to spread the good news. They were celebrating this victory of community care and defense when James Fields drove his car down Fourth Street, killing Heyer and injuring thirty-five others. Fourth Street, one of only two places to cross Charlottesville's pedestrian mall, was supposed to be closed for the day. In another institutional lapse, the road had been opened to vehicles.

There are two key lessons to draw here. The first is about the failures of various institutions—the University of Virginia, the police—to protect the groups they purport to serve in the face of both spectacularized and bureaucratized violence. As we have seen through numerous examples over the past several years, most recently the police killing of Stephon Clark in Sacramento, policing does not protect the many people of color murdered by police or the communities subjected to relentless and unnecessary harassment and surveillance.

Likewise, the university does not protect those paid as little as $7.25 per hour to keep it running, those saddled with unpayable debts upon graduation, or those gentrified out of their homes due to the university's expansion into surrounding neighborhoods.

But the second lesson to take away is the lesson about what does keep us safe: protection through solidarity with our most vulnerable communities. If our current institutions have failed us, then the case of August 12 gives us a roadmap to what institutions we should build to replace them: institutions that seek to work with and safeguard those most vulnerable to violence. August 12 teaches us, among so many other things, that locked doors don't make us safe. What will make us safe is stable and suitable housing, living wages, effective healthcare, and nutritious food built and advocated for through solidarity and partnerships.

Laura Goldblatt is the global studies postdoctoral fellow at the University of Virginia.

Michael Weinman

Aristotle on Charlottesville

'Mixed Actions' and Exercising Judgement on Violence

In the opening movement of Book 3 of his *Nicomachean Ethics,* Aristotle argues that, at bottom, each and every human being is responsible for essentially every action they undertake; put another way: there is nothing a human being does for which they ought not to be praised or blamed. This assertion, at the heart of his analysis of "voluntary and involuntary actions," is requisite for his "virtue ethics" to have any salience: if we are not responsible for actions, then we are not properly considered worthy of praise or blame for what we do, and if we are not so *properly* considered, then virtue and vice as attributes of the soul ("so-holdings" [*hexeis,* via Latin, "habits"] a misleading translation), don't capture anything real.

There's one very interesting exception to this generalized pronouncement. While Aristotle refuses to accept that there is any action undertaken by a human being that is not subject to praise or blame on account of either the actor (a) not knowing what they are doing or (b) acting under compulsion, he does acknowledge that there are some actions that are genuinely "mixed" actions. Such "mixed" actions are those that no sane person would choose for their own sake, but nevertheless are, under certain circumstances, chosen as the least bad course of action. As such, we cannot say that such actions are involuntary—they are chosen "under certain circumstances"—but we also cannot say they are voluntary simply since they would never be chosen for their own sake; hence, they are mixed, a mixture of voluntary and involuntary.

Why does this matter? It matters because the voluntariness of an action is a condition of our judgment of the actor who engages in that action. For a person who engages in such "mixed" action, committing an act we would normally find blameworthy, Aristotle says, we offer neither praise nor blame, but rather pity or pardon. For instance, if someone under the threat of physical harm or death from a tyrant, offers false testimony or harms an innocent, we surely do not praise the person, but neither do we blame them; rather, if we have judgment, we pardon them the transgression, in the belief that—now that the extreme circumstance has passed—this person will act in accordance with virtue, or at least not viciously. Or, perhaps, if the act was sufficiently heinous but clearly "mixed" (that is, not entirely voluntary), then maybe we do not pardon the person outright, but rather offer our pity for their circumstances. In such a case, they are not "cleared" of the offense, but they are not the object of blame either.

I think this analysis of "mixed" actions has a lot of salience as the collective response to the travesty in Charlottesville on Friday 11 and Saturday 12 of August continues to simmer. In particular, I think it is the most helpful lens through which to view and debate the moral and political judgment of counter-protesters who engage in violence, and especially those who are residents and citizens of Charlottesville itself.

Before offering that contribution, let me say that as someone who resided in Charlottesville in 2016,[1] as a Jew,[2] and most of

---

1   Polina Garaev, "While white nationalism erupts in the US, Germans protest racism and hatred," *i24NEWS*, August 17, 2017.

2   Alan Zimmerman, "In Charlottesville, the local Jewish community presses on," *Reform Judaism*, August 14, 2017.

all, as someone who expressed agreement with Charlottesville's Mayor Mike Signer's opposition to the removal of the Robert E. Lee statue,[3] I find, as many people do, much to say about what transpired. There's so much, indeed, that to my mind remains under-discussed: beginning with the July 2017 KKK rally in the recently renamed Justice Park,[4] which was an absolute disaster from a crowd control perspective and really ought to have prompted persons in and out of local and state government to do more to avert the disaster that followed a month later; but also the highly successful "take back the lawn" event[5] and other actions of healing and solidarity in Charlottesville in the weeks following August 11 and 12; and less brightly, the tumultuous and difficult to watch first city council meeting[6] after the riot and violence.

In short, there isn't enough time in the world to say what needs to be said about what happened, and the small city of Charlottesville and the surrounding community, the Commonwealth of Virginia, and the nation of my birth will have all their plate full with this for months to come, at least. For today, I hope to offer some food for thought for those who have been engaging in the most heated debate since the events of August 12 and especially since the controversy erupted about the "violence on many sides" response from President Donald Trump, and then the revision of

---

3 Michael Weinman, "Mayoral statements on Confederate memorials: Misrepresentation and misrecognition, yet again (part two)," *Public Seminar*, June 12, 2017.

4 Hawes Spencer and Matt Stevens, "23 arrested and tear gas deployed after a KKK rally in Virginia," *The New York Times*, July 8, 2017.

5 Debbie Elliot, "Torches replaced by candlelight as thousands gather for Charlottesville vigil," *NPR*, August 17, 2017.

6 Frances Robles, "Chaos breaks out at Charlottesville city council meeting," *The New York Times*, August 21, 2017.

that response on Monday 14, and then the revision of that revision on Tuesday 15. Namely: how are we to judge the counter-protesters who resorted to acts of violence? Or as I believe it is fairer to put it given my access to the thought process of some of those persons, how are we to judge the counter-protesters, especially those who reside in Charlottesville, who believed that under the circumstances, to refuse to meet violence with violence would be irresponsible?

One important caveat is required before I draw the perhaps now obvious conclusion I draw with reference to Aristotle's "mixed" actions analysis. Namely: in making the argument I will now make, I am not defending the thoughts or deeds of left-wing practitioners of direct action, often with anarcho-syndicalist[7] or Communist commitments, and often with an open acceptance of violence as a means to counter what they believe to be the inherent violence of the international capitalist order. In recent days, it has become habitual to refer to such actors as antifascist action, or antifa. Antifa of course exists, and there is a strong overlap between antifa and the left-wing practitioners of direct action. They are not the same, the same way that the AfD and the NDP in Germany or UKIP and the BNP in England (England, especially) are not the same, and it is important to understand all these nuances, as Peter Beinart tries to do in a long-form piece for *The Atlantic*.[8]

Thinking, now, not about those who so identify as part of a movement, but rather about individual actors who joined with neighbors to respond to the presence of people who often traveled great distances to communicate a message of hate and

7   Rudolf Rocker, "Anarcho-syndicalism: Theory and practice," *The Anarchist Library*, April 26, 2009.

8   Peter Beinart, "The rise of the violent left," *The Atlantic*, September 2017.

intimidation, I pose the question of the application of Aristotle's analysis to the instant case. In face of the events, we ask not the blanket universal question: is it blameworthy to voluntarily engage in violence in the streets—against state or non-state actors in a democratic society—in order to advance or defend a political point of view? Here the obvious answer is yes. But it is the wrong question, because we are not thinking about "voluntary actions" at all. Rather, those who came out in response to Richard Spencer and Jason Kessler (and by all means read up on their words and deeds over the past year for a few minutes in order to assess their perspective) and those they gathered, and found themselves in circumstances where for whatever reason law enforcement personnel had abdicated the monopoly on violence, and therefore engaged in a recognizably mixed action: they chose, under certain circumstances, to engage in actions that (we judge) no sane person would choose, simply and without qualification. As such, even though engaging in physical intimidation in insisting that people leave the streets is something that we could not possibly praise, it also is reasonable to judge that it doesn't merit blame either. With "mixed" actions, there is a non-excluded middle between virtuous (praiseworthy) and vicious (blameworthy). And that is precisely where, in my judgment, these actions fall. One might consider the counter-protesters to have done something it would be wrong to choose to do but as good as necessary in such circumstances; in this case you would pardon them. Or you might deem their actions as sufficiently unworthy of choice that you can only find your way to pity them in their circumstances. What, Aristotle's analysis suggests, you cannot reasonably judge is that they merit your blame. Especially if you are judging from afar, and under very different circumstances.

MICHAEL WEINMAN

Michael Weinman is professor of philosophy at Bard College Berlin. He primarily works on ancient Greek thought, political philosophy, and their intersection. His most recent book The Parthenon and Liberal Education, *co-authored with Geoff Lehman, was published in the* SUNY Series in Ancient Greek Philosophy *in March 2018. Originally published in* Public Seminar, *August 28, 2017.*

Maria Bucur

Remembering Romanian Fascism; Worrying About America

Losing Our Moral Compass Between Past and Future

My father left Romania for the United States in 1983 to escape a dictatorship and give his children the opportunity to develop their talents and follow their intellectual ambition. In the eighties, living under the regime of Nicolae Ceaușescu was unbearable. We lived "bonsai lives," as a friend of mine calls them: each of us potted and trimmed just so we wouldn't develop wildly and freely without the Communist Party's approval. If you followed the "correct" path, you might be able to arrive at a secure job, with food on the table, a pension, an apartment, maybe a car and a telephone, or even cheap vacations with colleagues. If you insisted on asking questions, reading the wrong things, and turning on Radio Free Europe, you risked being taken off that road towards potted security; you might spend the rest of your life working in a crappy factory job in a third rate city—that is, if you weren't thrown in jail. Though some scholars describe it as "the exception," Romania was a textbook example of state socialism, of what a one-party state does to hope, ambition, love of learning, and the spirit of entrepreneurship. The legacy of living under a system of institutionalized corruption, pervasive suspicion, and fear is losing one's moral compass.

Living under Ceaușescu was in some ways like living with Donald Trump as president. There was a lot of nationalist swagger, posturing, and boasting about independence from the Soviets. When Ceaușescu refused to send troops into Czechoslovakia in 1968 as part of the Warsaw Pact crackdown on student protests, people of my parents' generation started to look at him as a hero: the man who stood up to Leonid Brezhnev. Ceaușescu's obsession with flaunting Romania's independence and greatness, along with his own cult of personality, started to swell like a cancer in the seventies. Cabinet members were made to declare over and over, on radio, in newspapers, and on TV, their love and admiration for the Great Leader. It was mandated that his portrait hang in every classroom and government office. He did not golf, but would pose with all the bears he killed on his hunting expeditions.

Eventually, even the Soviets grew tired of Ceaușescu's posturing. After Mikhail Gorbachev came to power and signaled to other Eastern Europe countries that the Soviet Union would not use military force to preserve communism beyond its borders, Romania and Albania were the only countries where the leadership insisted on remaining as dictatorial as they had been up to then. With the exception of a handful who dared to criticize the regime from inside, most people chose to put their heads down and live in fear. That was when my dad decided he had had enough and left Romania, risking his life.

Though my father had joined the Communist Party in the sixties—he, like others, was supportive of Ceaușescu's independence from the Soviet Union—he had realized his mistake by the mid-eighties. To his credit, he understood what a democracy was and brought his adolescent children away from that place of moral equivalence, fear, and oppression. He gave me the opportunity to learn to differentiate between bowing to party propaganda and becoming educated through uncensored journalism, between bigotry clothed in "free speech" arguments and criticism of xenophobia, racism, and sexism. By taking us out of that toxic environment, my dad enabled my brother and me to make moral choices with all the wisdom that living under a dictatorship teaches you: freedom is a privilege—not just a right—and you must exercise it responsibly, with care for all around you.

Because the Communist Party tightly controlled information, I was ignorant of fascism in the eighties, ignorant of its deep roots in Romania and in my family. The Communist regime talked about it as if it had been something foreign to Romania's history, rather than an intimate part of many families' pasts. There existed neither historical research nor publications on the homegrown Legion of the Archangel Michael and the movement it gave rise to, the Iron Guard. The fascist regime that governed Romania during the Second World War, led by Ion Antonescu, was called "Hitlerist," as if it did not comprise Romanian men who were racist nationalists before allying with the Nazis.

I learned a great deal more about Romanian fascism when I started travelling to post-Communist Romania in the mid-nineties with an American passport to study the roots of Romania's eugenics movement. In 1995 my grandmother let it slip that my grandfather had joined the Iron Guard in the 1930s. He was dead by the mid-nineties, so I got very little detail beyond the claim that he was just an opportunist. Others since have told me about familial ties to the Legion of the Archangel Michael, consistently referring to it as "just" a Christian nationalist movement. Why "just"? One is not "just" a member of a fascist movement. One chooses to become part of a hate group bent on the elimination of another group based on their biology, and one must contend with the implications thereof. Just like one cannot claim to be "just" a

Trump supporter because the man promised to "Make America Great Again" while conveniently ignoring the president's racism and misogyny prior to and since the election.

In the nineties a growing chorus of politicians, writers, and historians in Romania began to tout the homegrown fascists as patriots because they had opposed Communism, something that in and of itself signified moral superiority. Monuments went up to Ion Antonescu and the paramilitary bands of fascists who fought against the Communist takeover in the forties. Cultural organizations were named after members of the Nazi Party. Fascists were declared patriots and martyrs because they had fought the Soviets and lost.

In the past fifteen years, however, the pendulum has swung back. Vocal criticism of Antonescu's murderous government has made possible the passing of legislation that forbids naming public institutions and streets after symbols, persons, or organizations connected with the wartime regime. Statues dedicated to any such figures have been taken down or relocated to the private property of willing owners. I can't say that Romania's moral compass has been fully repaired, but these changes give me a great deal of hope that such extremist attitudes can be overcome.

Today I am a 48-year-old woman with two teenage boys, living in Southern Indiana and teaching at a public university. And, until recently, I felt lucky to be away from the extremism I encountered far too often on my frequent trips back to Romania. But 45 miles from me, in Paoli, lives Matthew Heinbach, who organized a major fascist demonstration in Charlottesville, Virginia, on the campus of one of the oldest institutions of higher learning in the United States, a university built on the foundations of Enlightenment thought, with all its complicated legacies of slavery and belief in the freedom of thought.

At the impromptu press conference Heinbach held after the terrorist attack by car, he claimed victory for the alt-right and criticized the police for failing to protect the fascists' right to free speech and assembly. He wore a T-shirt bearing a portrait of Corneliu Zelea Codreanu—the leader of the fascist movement to which my grandfather belonged—and the word *prezent* in capital letters. In Romanian this word means both "present/now" and "ready." It is the response that members of a military unit give their leader when lined up in formation. I see this choice as a direct signal to other fascists that he is present and ready to assume his duties towards this movement, as well as a direct threat to those who understand the history of fascism.

In light of recent events, can I continue to think about the past in the same way as before? As a historian, the adage "history is condemned to repeat itself" has always seemed nonsensical to me. History cannot repeat itself; it is a flowing river of ever-changing context. But people like Heinbach want to see it repeat itself. He admires Codreanu and probably wishes to see a revival of the fascist cells, labor camps, and legionary stores the fascist movement built in Romania.

The challenge before us today is to insist that we cannot and should not allow history to repeat itself. To do so will require that we educate ourselves about the impact radical right- and left-wing ideologies had on the societies where these ideas became reality; to think responsibly about the privileges we still hold in this country as citizens of neither a Communist nor a fascist regime; and to call out the alt-right and their allies for what they are: a dangerous force undermining our children's future. If America loses its moral compass, where will I take my children?

Maria Bucur is the John W. Hill professor of East European history and gender studies at Indiana University, Bloomington. She has written on the history of eugenics, memory and war, and citizenship in Eastern Europe. Her book The Century of Women: How Women Have Transformed the World since 1900 *was published by Rowman and Littlefield in May 2018. Originally published in* Public Seminar, *September 3, 2017.*

Marcus McCullough

Thinking After Charlottesville

A Meditation on More of the Same

I kinda feel bad . . . I feel like something is wrong with me. Why don't I feel this? Where is my outrage? Everyone else seems to be feeling it. What the hell is wrong with me?

Oh, I think I've got it: I ain't that moved . . . because I ain't surprised.

That dreadful Saturday in Charlottesville, Virginia will be etched in history, and rightfully so. A group of conservative right-wing demonstrators gathered and marched on the University of Virginia campus to protest the removal of statues honoring figures who fought for the Confederacy during the American Civil War. Trumpeting the noble cause of preserving history, these demonstrators marched with the message that removing said statues was tantamount to erasing a part of American history worthy of preservation.

Truly—so goes the ploy—this group set out to exercise our constitutional right to peaceful assembly and protest. However, unlike other peaceful demonstrations, such as those under the humane cry "Black Lives Matter!" or those occurring on NFL football fields this season, this demonstration was anything but peaceful. Why? Because brandishing weapons, particularly military-grade assault firearms, makes violence an essential component of the event's DNA. The guns in this rally were not symbols of defense and protection, just as they were not symbols of defense and protection in 2009 when individuals strapped with firearms[1] showed up outside town halls and speeches of then-President Barack Obama. These guns are wielded as a threat; these are symbols of assault, violence, and fear. Add to this the lit tiki torches and the slur-ridden chanting and you have quite a demonstration—a *violent* one.

Surely—we assure ourselves—the police would be present at such a gathering. Surely, they would be in riot gear with their militarized weaponry (like they are as soon as the humane cry "Black lives matter!" is raised). Better yet, the National Guard would be present! Yes, of course! This is a college campus—a public one— so this is undeniably under their jurisdiction. They were dispatched to help de-segregate schools in Virginia and other places, coming forth to protect vulnerable students, so surely they *must* be dispatched to this situation, seeing as how students' lives— young, promising students' lives—could be endangered. Surely!

But there were no police. There was no National Guard. There was no militarized force at all attending to this inherently violent, *definitely not peaceful,* demonstration.

So let me get this straight: the presence of military-grade guns and fire-and-hate-filled chanting is not enough to bring in police but one prophetic cry—"Black lives matter!"—is enough and then some?

To my great dismay, I was not surprised. Nor was I was enraged, shocked, or frankly, even appalled at the blatant displays of white supremacist ideology. How could I be surprised? Enraged? How could I feel a surge of such powerful emotion when this felt like nothin' new under the sun?

---

1 "Man with assault rifle attends Obama protest," *NBC News*, August 18, 2009.

Consider that for me anger—rage—has been a bosom buddy my entire life. As a young Black man raised in a very socially— and racially—conscious household, church, and community, I have always been more than aware of my people's troubles and the cries that have repeatedly been muffled, usually in an effort to protect white sensibilities ("All lives matter"). For as long as I can remember, it has made me angry. But I had to suppress it just enough to function, let alone succeed, in spaces dominated by whiteness. Thus, my anger and I learned to dance delicately. We have always danced in a manner reflective of a near-perfect symbiosis, we have danced a dance of energy and passion restrained just enough to be "tasteful" or "palatable" to onlookers. But the passion, the fire, was never lost; it was merely channeled. And as I matriculated in my manhood, my Blackness, and my discipleship of Jesus, I began to lay claim to righteous indignation, even to sanctify it in my own heart, just as much an expression of God within me as the Holy Spirit and a love for my father's grits on a Sunday morning. This rage is and always has been a part of me, and it is a part of my God as well.

So that day, when I didn't feel it—any of it—I had to figure something was off.

I was curious, nagged, confused. But not shocked, not outraged. I had to take stock of what others were saying and doing.

Many of my friends seemed to feel what I was not feeling, at least according to multiple social media posts. Many of them articulated their feelings—their sorrow, their shock, their rage—so well, so powerfully. I felt strange and alienated not feeling any of the rage that I saw expressed by others. Perhaps I felt some sadness about the events, but not much. What did bother me, increasingly, was that a fire was raging and it seemed I could not feel any of the heat.

Then came the moment I realized that I had grown numb.

The lack of law enforcement in the face of an overtly threatening demonstration led by white supremacists felt familiar. It seemed that to be surprised would mean that you'd been lucky enough to be blind to what it's like to be Black in this country, to carry and live the weight of Black history and Black present. Perhaps, well-meaning and justice-oriented though it may be, white shock and outrage at the happenings, the news coverage, the photos, the rhetoric, just made me think of another repetition without change. It made me think about the similar reaction from white allies when civil rights marchers were violently attacked on Edmund Pettus Bridge on that Bloody Sunday of 1965. Much has changed, sure, but much has remained the same.

Although initially it seemed the shock and horror reaction was pervasive, in the days that followed my Facebook feed began to reflect Black people (mostly my age, thirty-something or close to it) expressing the same thought that dominated my psyche: *now* you are surprised?? Why?? Black people have been speaking this reality for generations (no, not years, *generations*)! Here is *yet another instance* that left me saying, "What if there were no video?" Those of you who acted or felt surprised, did you think we were making things up? For generations?! No, wait, I get it...you musta actually believed that all lives actually matter—why else would the prophet's cry of "Black lives matter!" be so offensive to you? Somehow *this* event moved you, whereas the videos of Philando Castile, Eric Garner, Walter Scott, Sandra Bland, and others did not? *Now* you are moved?? Why?!?

The conclusion I came to is one of those that some folks might find "unpalatable" but it is too damned familiar to deny it, and it's been denied and avoided and elided as many times as it's been con-firmed—more times than can be counted. Why did this demon-stration incite such moral outrage on behalf of so many? Was it the affront to Black personhood? Was it the outright celebration of vio-lent suppression of Black lives? No. What was it then?

A white woman was killed. A white female counter-demonstrator was struck and killed by a car that was driven by an enraged white man sympathetic to the original demonstrators (how quickly did the Mentally Ill Card get played in defense of white male terroristic behavior *this* time?). That's right: the fire of public (white) outrage was quickly fanned into a blaze when a white woman was killed. Though not calloused about this young woman's death, I cannot help but see the public outcry as representative of the long-tired truth that white bodies are regarded as intrinsically more valuable than black bodies.

I have lived long enough to know this narrative: the white woman (especially young and pretty) has a body—I mean, a life—considered more valuable than anything else, especially to white men. Leaving aside the deeply problematic elements of patriarchal ownership and control often inherent in the val-uation of women's bodies, these bodies and these lives are still regarded as most worthy of protection in the present system, dominated as it is by white male interests. Protecting white female personhood and progeny is paramount.

And then we have the perpetrator.

Though not surprised, I am constantly amazed by how strongly society protects white males and defends their behavior. Whether a brawl on the NASCAR track or a "good, Christian young man" slay-ing moviegoers in Colorado, we have perfected the craft of explain-ing away certain behaviors if a white male commits them. Hence, a situation of white men in open and armed defiance of the U.S. government in Oregon[2] can end in peace but peaceful demonstrations of Black people are treated like there are "wars and rumors of wars" (Matthew 24:6)—yes, this is a peace that surpasses all understanding, because it doesn't make any sense. Returning to Charlottesville, even the father of the deceased young woman spoke about the perpetrator as if he were merely a foolish, misled young man, not as a murderer and a terrorist (ey yo…did they play the Mentally Ill Card in defense of white male terroristic behavior yet?). I guess "(white) boys will be boys" is still, and will continue to be, more acceptable than "Black lives matter!"

I guess that is why prophets of the latter are forced to be the "voice crying in the wilderness" (John 1:23) while the pundit of the former gets to tweet comfortably from the White House.

I do wonder, though, did folks go out of the way to humanize this terrorist like they did the Aurora, Colorado movie theater shooter? Remember how this young man was described as a quiet, humble, Christian young man, active in his church? Do you recall that this was mere days after he massacred twelve people watching a Batman movie in 2012? Remember how many still designate this as a "mass murder" and not a terror attack, despite guns and bombs found in his home?

Oh? Charlottesville was different? They did *not* try to humanize the terroristic white male this time? Why not?

It is nearly impossible not to view it in the light of race, in light of whose bodies matter: a young white woman with no children was killed. This is paramount to everything else.

---

2 Courtney Sherwood and Kirk Johnson, "Bundy brothers acquitted in takeover of Oregon wildlife refuge," *The New York Times,* October 27, 2006.

This song and dance is not new to any who are oppressed or marginalized: labels are applied differently depending upon who is involved, depending upon who the perpetrator and the victim are. If there is anything that seems to irk white America enough to avoid sympathizing with awful, even terroristic, white male behavior, it is the killing of a (young) white woman. That seems to be the line, that seems to be what sparks the outrage, that seems to be the determining factor. It is not whether the alleged perpetrator had a gun or not—certainly, it isn't whether there was a child in the car or not—it is whether or not white men, and certainly white women, are harmed.

I was not enraged by the happenings in Charlottesville because I was not surprised by the events in Charlottesville. Neither was I surprised by all of the outrage and explaining away that soon attended the whole fiasco. By now, I know very well how this society works. I did not need to preach on Charlottesville the next day because I had already preached on such things and I knew I would eventually preach on such matters again—likely sooner than I would prefer. Unlike some others, I did not feel an urgent need to cry out about this matter on my social media status, not because it is unimportant, but because like an ancient prophet I am perplexed about what words to use and what good they would be. Like Isaiah, perhaps, I was lost, asking, "What shall I cry?" (Isaiah 40:6). What have I to add? We already know well how Black voices are a threat but white voices are welcomed—even when brandishing guns, hiding behind flag idolatry, and voting in a 53 percent majority for the sitting U.S. president.

I get it, I done been got it a long time ago. I been knew that white liberal outrage is selectively fierce and fiercely selective— I learned that as a graduate student at Harvard. I knew before all the subsequent "peaceful demonstrations" that bastions of (white) liberalism would have folks squad up (i.e., rally together) to counter-demonstrate while continuing to comfortably abide in racist cities with an abysmal imbalance of power. I knew that as a nine-year resident of Boston, a city that is so racist and lopsided that its own paper pointed out in a recent series of articles that even though the city boasts a majority population of people of color, the power, access, and money still sits in white hands. I was not fooled in graduate school, I was not fooled in Boston, I am not fooled by much of anything. And I damn sure was not surprised by anything regarding that Saturday in Charlottesville. I may not have grown up in the Confederate Battle Flag South, but I have been in enough spaces, north, south, east, and west, to recognize when white supremacy merely enlists a new crop of soldiers.

So, no, I am not surprised. Why should I be? And if I am angry, it is more at the theatre of social outrage. Because all it did was put it right under my nose that people still don't get it. All it did was remind me whose lives *actually* matter (big hint: *it's not all!*). That fateful day was one of preaching to the choir, and the sermon was old, and the hearers continued to wallow in their sin. So I will let the prophet move me but not Charlottesville enrage me—it can't.

I just ain't surprised.

Reverend Marcus Toure B. McCullough is a pastor of the African Methodist Episcopal Church. He is a graduate of Morehouse College, and has earned masters degrees in divinity and sacred theology from Harvard Divinity School and Boston University School of Theology.

PART 2

Vaughn A. Booker

The False God of Nationalism

Speaking on the first black-owned radio station in the U.S. in 1953, Reverend Dr. Martin Luther King, Jr. preached on "The False God of Nationalism." In the sermon, preached at Ebenezer Baptist Church and broadcast on Atlanta-based WERD radio station, King framed nationalism as a "new religion" that once had German and Italian preachers in Hitler and Mussolini, and identified the preachers of America's "my country right or wrong" nationalism as "the McCarthys and the Jenners, the advocators of white supremacy, and the America first movements." Because of the popularity of these nationalistic preachers, King lamented, "We live in an age when it is almost heresy to affirm the brotherhood of man." As a mainline black Protestant church minister in the early years of the Cold War, King's concern was that he lived in an age where people had "turned away from the eternal God of the universe, and decided to worship at the shrine of the god of nationalism."

Six years after this nation dedicated a monument to King in its capital in 2011, Americans face a new nationalism that is likely to inhabit the government for at least four years. The proponents of this nationalism, who occasionally speak of a concept of "economic nationalism," imitate a populism that claims a concern for all those "left out" by the new economy. They claim a priority for bringing "the forgotten" rural voters employment opportunities. They promise to disentangle our nation from violent foreign military affairs that have caused the displacement of millions.

But domestically, these new nationalists appoint economic advisors and cabinet members who prioritize corporate profit and efficient labor practices over the protections of a labor force that many mega-businesses ultimately wish to reduce and automate. Internationally, they have expressed romantic admiration for practices of "enhanced interrogation" considered torture. They have aligned with strongmen leaders in Russia, Turkey, and the Philippines, all nations with governments that practice little regard for human rights and show that they are more than willing to be militaristic, even if that means violence against their own citizens. Rhetorically, they claim that the millions more who voted against nationalism were comprised mainly of black and brown illegal voters, promote long-standing policy efforts of voter disenfranchisement, and dismiss protest and policy efforts to reform policing and criminal punishment in America. The new nationalism shows no evidence of concern to thwart what King identified as the triple evils of poverty, militarism, and racism. Rather, it appears ready to benefit from all three.

While it may feel peculiar in this present moment to experience the successful, rapid spread of new nationalistic ideas in the United States, these movements have been gaining visibility throughout the Western world. The displacement of peoples into and within predominantly white Western countries from Latin America, for reasons of lack of economic opportunity and safety, as well as the influx of refugees into Western European nations and the United States from parts of Africa and the Middle East, have bolstered arguments, political movements, and enterprising politicians who believe these migrations signal existential threats to their country's national security. In response to the people of color whose presence threatens ideals of civilization and ethnic purity, there are more extremist and visible forms of these arguments that advocate explicit ethnonationalism. In the case of long-standing white nationalist movements in Europe and the United States, these arguments also maintain and extend familiar anti-Semitic discourses of an impending "replacement" of whites with Anglo-Saxon heritage by nonwhite, non-Christian others.

Migrants and refugees of color in the United States pose these threats because, unlike in King's time, there is no enforced legal and de facto system of Jim Crow segregation to police minority travel and interracial intimacy. No longer are there explicit racial codes to create and maintain strong cultural divisions and, most importantly, to prevent white people from falling in love and reproducing with people of color. Gatherings like the "Unite the Right" rally on August 11 and 12, 2017, in Charlottesville, Virginia, journalistic profiles of the newest generation of prominent white supremacists, and vibrant nationalist online communities that organized hashtags like #whitegenocide to trend during the 2016 election cycle, reflect pervasive contentions that these global movements of people pose threats to the stability and supremacy of nationalist (cultural, religious, and racial) identities.

For King, the fear was that nationalism was once again leading to war—this time, plunging the world into "the abyss of atomic destruction." Believing that "nationalism must give way to internationalism," King preached further, "It is nationalism perverted into chauvinism and isolationism that I am condemning. One cannot worship this false god of nationalism and the God of Christianity at the same time." For King, Americans must choose whom they serve, and he asked of his audience a series of questions about their ultimate commitments: "Will we continue to serve the false god that places absolute national sovereignty first or will we serve the false god of imperialistic greed or will we serve the God who makes love the key which unlocks the door of peace and security? Will we continue to serve the false god of racial prejudice or will we serve the God who made of one blood all men to dwell upon the face of the earth?"

King called for the presence of "prophetic voices to cry out against the false god of nationalism." Such voices may have to fight legal, political, social, and cultural battles that those in the Reconstruction era, in the early twentieth century, in mid-century, and in the post-civil rights eras believed they had won for posterity. As a liberal minister, King emerged from a generation of preachers who practiced a novel form of social activism from their pulpits while also developing interracial and interreligious networks. He was one of many inheritors of activist traditions who knew that progress required both sophistication and endurance, because oppressive governance is both sophisticated and more than ready to endure political pushback to secure social dominance for generations.

How will we contend with this new nationalism, in the memory and spirit of King and other nonviolent activist women and men? What is it about our own professional passions, or professional calling, that will lend to making our nation and our world less unfair, less violent, and more loving?

Vaughn A. Booker is an assistant professor in the department of religion in African and African American studies at Dartmouth College. His specialization is the historical study of African American religions in the twentieth century. Originally published in Public Seminar, *January 9, 2018.*

Sanford Schram

Russia Is Our Friend

The Alt-Right, Trump, and the Transformation of the
Republican Party

Considering recent events, there are troubling developments
occurring behind the scenes underscoring how Donald Trump's
relationship to the alt-right is transforming the Republican
Party—in more ways than one. There were already signs that the
Republican Party had gone beyond dog-whistling[1] about race
to being the party of white nationalists who use a megaphone to
champion their cause of promoting white lives over all others. It
also had gone from being the party that railed against Communist
Russia to the party that stands by while their president shares
secrets[2] with the autocratic kleptocracy that now rules Russia.

Race and Russia might seem to be two different issues. After
all, one is more domestic and the other foreign. But, thanks
to the rise of the alt-right and the critical role they have played
in Trump's political ascendancy, they are in fact deeply related.

Recently, it was reported that several dozen torch-bearing demonstrators appeared in Charlottesville, Virginia,[3] on
a Saturday night chanting, "You will not replace us," "Rus-

---

1 Xaxnar, "This is way beyond dog-whistling. This is Trump-eting. Heckuva job GOP,"
Daily Kos, August 9, 2016.

2 Peter Baker and Julie Hirschfeld Davis, "Trump defends sharing information on ISIS
threat with Russia," *The New York Times*, May 16, 2017.

3 Noweasels, "Torch-wielding white supremacists march on Charlottesville," *Daily Kos*,
May 14, 2017.

sia is our friend," and "Blood and soil." Among those chanting was Richard Spencer, the putative leader of what has come to be called the alt-right, i.e., white nationalists committed to standing up for those whom they see as "real Americans." The alt-right was a critical part of Trump's constituency in the 2016 election. They not only helped him win the presidency but have also proven resolute in their support. That support remains in spite of Trump's missteps that affected items on the alt-right's own agenda, like banning Muslims, limiting illegal immigration from Mexico, cracking down on black crime, improving relations with Mother Russia, putting America first in trade, and avoiding foreign entanglements in the Middle East and elsewhere. Trump is committed to defending them from those demonized "others" and they are sticking with him.

The image of a torch-bearing crowd marching in the name of white nationalism, if not white supremacy, seemed intentionally staged to be reminiscent of Nazis marching in support of Adolf Hitler. The racism of this movement is transparent; they were there to protest the removal of a statue of Robert E. Lee, the commander of the Confederate Army. Their racism, however, was also reflective of the more diluted forms of racial resentment that animated the broader base of whites who supported Trump. Altogether, the various strains of racialized support for Trump made his constituency more about race than class,[4] and—at a minimum—meant that economic anxieties associated with the failures of the neoliberalized economy were being focused through a racial lens. Trump's populism was more about race than class.

---

[4] German Lopez, "Survey: The poor white working class was, if anything, more likely than the rich to vote for Clinton," *Vox*, May 9, 2017.

While the racism of the Republican Party has been increasing in prominence for some time,[5] the movement that coalesced behind Trump has both made this much more explicit and remade the Republican Party in the process.

The rise of white nationalism in the Republican Party however has also been producing a Republican reevaluation of American relations with Russia. The alt-right has led the way on this front as well. The alt-right's cock-eyed view of racial relations in a globalizing world has a special place for Russia right at the center,[6] as a leader of white nationalism worldwide. This racist affinity for Russia has infected the Republican base more generally in part as less racist conservatives have left the party to be replaced by white nationalists and others who are not concerned about the warming to Russia.

As a craven opportunist in both business and life, for years Trump has been shopping for a political constituency, ultimately coming home to his worst racist instincts and making a Faustian bargain with the alt-right. He aligned himself with leaders of that movement, especially Steve Bannon at the far-right news outlet *Breitbart*,[7] who now is a senior advisor in Trump's White House. Fanning the flames of white anxiety more generally, Trump rode the tidal wave of racial resentment to the White House to impose a kleptocratic authoritarian-style presidency. It was a fraught bargain to say the least.

The Republican Party's leadership has done the same with Trump—tolerating his outrageous lies, his unethical behavior,

5   Joseph Lowndes, "Why are GOP contenders reviving racist rhetoric?" *HuffPost*, March 17, 2012.

6   Casey Michel, "How America's right-wing fell in love with Putin and Moscow," *Alternet*, March 8, 2017.

7   "Steve Bannon strategy helped bring Trump to victory on election day," *Breitbart*, 17 December, 2016.

and reprehensible policy initiatives. They have done all of this in the name of a president who will support their massive transfer of wealth upward while gutting the welfare state and deregulating the economy. Trump's extremely corporate-friendly cabinet has reassured them that their bargain may be worth it.

As recent events highlight, Trump's relationship to the alt-right is remaking the Republican Party as surrogates for President Vladimir Putin's Russia. It is surely shocking to think that the Republican Party—the party of anti-Communism and of the Red Scare—has shown so little resistance to this about-face with regard to Russia. Certainly, it's true that Putin's Russia is not communist, but there is nearly as little to recommend today's Russian autocracy to Republicans as the communism of the prior regime. Nonetheless, Republicans have stood largely silent while Trump has played footsie with Putin.

The spinelessness of the Republican Party is evidenced by the reaction to Trump's decision to fire FBI Director James Comey. They stood silent when Trump announced—contrary to his own press office and surrogates, including the vice president—that he terminated Comey because he had become frustrated with the FBI investigation regarding whether or not he colluded with the Russians to influence the very election that put him in the White House. This blatant announcement of his own attempt to obstruct an investigation into his possible complicity with the Russians did little more than raise a few eyebrows among Republican leadership. There were no expressions of outrage.

Now, most recently and perhaps most controversially, the Republican Party leadership has failed to condemn Trump irresponsibly divulging to the Russian foreign minister top secret information that has likely endangered national security.[8] And on top of that we now learn that Republicans are mulling over how to respond to reports that Trump asked Comey to drop his investigation of fired National Security Advisor Michael Flynn regarding his possible collusion with the Russians.

The rise of the alt-right has helped Trump win the presidency and has brought both race and Russia to the forefront of U.S. politics in deeply disturbing ways. This diabolical combination has led to the remarkable transformation of the Republican Party into a party of white nationalists willing to stand by silently while Trump and Putin impose their authoritarian kleptocratic regimes on the countries they rule. They stand by while Trump acts irresponsibly, unpredictably, and unilaterally, in his collaboration with Russia on matters that affect the U.S. domestically and internationally.

With friends like these, the American people don't need enemies.

Sanford Schram is professor of political science at Hunter College, where he also teaches public policy in Roosevelt House.

---

8   Jordan Fabian, "Trump: 'Great meeting' with Russian officials," *The Hill*, May 16, 2017.

Jeffrey C. Goldfarb

Being There, Separate and Unequal

Charlottesville in the Mediated Public Sphere

We are all in Charlottesville. We have been there before, and during, and will be there after the events of August 11 and 12, 2017. And there's no exit. The white supremacy and racism, supported by state power, monumentalized in words and stone, and resisted through all imaginable means, started with colonial settlement (before Charlottesville there was Jamestown),[1] and there are no signs that this is ending soon. The struggles for alternatives to the reprehensible persists,[2] as does the project of squelching alternatives, demonstrated by the repeatedly equivocal responses to Charlottesville by the president of the United States.

We are all there, fascist and anti-fascist, racist and anti-racist, "the united right" defending the Robert E. Lee monument, and those who protested their defense and their aggressive racist and anti-Semitic slogans and actions. And among the protesters, both those who make a strong distinction between the ideals of the founders of the American republic and the history and legacies of racism and slavery, and those who see the latter as an extension of the former in Charlottesville.[3]

---

1 Mindy Fullilove, Robert Fullilove, William Morrish, and Robert Sember, "Before Charlottesville there was Jamestown," *Public Seminar*, August 28, 2017.

2 Andrew Boyer, "What we really learned in Charlottesville," *Public Seminar*, November 9, 2017.

3 Keval Bhatt, "Subverting the symbols of white supremacy: The wolf and the fox," *Public Seminar*, October 17, 2017.

My theoretically informed observation: we are actually there much more than we realize. My political concern: we aren't there together. We are there isolated in our mediated silos, and this has significant political consequences.

While only a small number of people involved in the Charlottesville events were physically present, the rest of us were also directly involved through our mediated experience. Such is the nature of media events.

For much of my life, my presence at such events has been televisual. When I was a kid, I remember my intimate connection with the Kennedy assassination, as well as his inauguration. I had a personal relationship with J.F.K. These encounters were much more real than when I physically caught a glimpse of him as he motored through my hometown on the campaign trail, and again in lower Manhattan when he helicoptered into Battery Park for an official ceremony, and I was on a school trip.

You were all also involved in the attacks of 9/11. You saw the same video clips of the jets striking the World Trade Center. From around the globe, you watched the buildings collapse and the world change, and even those of you who are too young to remember directly have been there in retrospect, as these clips replay not just on television but on our computerized devices.

Joshua Meyrowitz's classic book, *No Sense of Place,* which combines the critical insights of Marshall McLuhan and Erving Goffman, provides an explanation for how such mediated involvement is personal involvement. As the electronic media extend our senses of hearing and seeing, our mediated interaction constitutes our social reality, and the sense of place (and time) is challenged, if not lost. For better and for worse, the distinctive places of the private and public, near and far, then and now, formal and informal, authoritative and democratic, men and women, black and white, and adults and children, Meyrowitz shows, have been broken down with the development of radio and television. The digital revolution radicalizes this.

Let's note that there are both positive and negative consequences to mediated experience. There is no longer distant suffering. That which occurs in a refugee camp on the other side of the world also happens on our phones, along with more mundane updates from our nearest and dearest. Men's "locker room talk" can no longer be confined to the locker room. Police brutality is no longer the exclusive experience of the brutes and the brutalized. Also the distinct contributions, responsibilities, and prerogatives of parties, professions, the sciences and the arts, universities, and religious institutions, among many others, are harder to maintain, as it is increasingly difficult to protect children from experiencing the depravity of adults.

This loss of a distinct sense of time and place very much applies to Charlottesville. The media made it relatively easy for a discrete number of extremists to see each other in mass and to be seen by others, and they thus became very real for themselves and for us. Who and how many they represented is far from certain. The way the U.S. president, arguably the most powerful person in the world responded,[4] was then profoundly important. Also very important is how we, who were there, respond, both at the time of the extremist demonstration and in its aftermath.

We present ourselves to each other and define the situation of our daily life through mediated interactions. We find out about events such as those in Charlottesville on Twitter and Facebook,

---

4   Leonard A. Williams, "On Trump's response to Charlottesville: Political encounters and ideological evasions," *Public Seminar*, August 25, 2017.

as we keep up to date on the latest developments and commentaries, and exchange information and commentary. We see them on TV. We hear them on radio. We turn to our phones as things are happening, and return on YouTube and podcasts, and in reading books and articles. In a very real way, we are there as we pay attention, and continue being there through paying attention, observing the images of those young, clean cut men, carrying firearms, chanting their despicable chants, along with the outraged response of the good citizens of the town and of our global village, and the provocative responses of the president. We experience all this directly. In the same way that those of us of a certain age were there in Dallas when the president was shot and at ground zero on 9/11.

We are in the middle of it.

But there is a big difference between then and now. Media events of the recent past, in the age of television, often fostered solidarity and supported a common public experience. In turn, these collective experiences supported democracy, as I have explained in a review essay[5] reconsidering how the classic books, *Media Events* by Daniel Dayan and Elihu Katz and *The Structural Transformation of the Public Sphere* by Jürgen Habermas, illuminate the present crisis. My conclusion:

> There are multiple publics that are centered into a Sphere of Publics, which attract various degrees of attention significantly broadened by ceremonial television. The media events that Dayan and Katz consider demonstrate this . . . Those who observe, talk about, and act in response to such events make up

---

5 Jeffrey C. Goldfarb, "Solidarity, and the rise and fall of the public sphere: A review of Daniel Dayan and Elihu Katz's media events," *Public Seminar*, April 18, 2017.

the broadest of publics. They take part in many other publics, but these media events create broad central publics to which they all have a connection. It is that connection that we are now missing, it would seem. This suggests a crisis in solidarity, along with a destructive transformation of the spheres of publics.

In an earlier media era, when television was king, the overwhelming majority of the population was tuned in, and under certain circumstances took part in ritualized media events, focused on the assassination, the inauguration, the Olympic games, and the like. The daily flow of media broadcasting was disrupted, all channels focused on the event. A mass audience experienced it together, in the same way. The united experience constituted through interactions, including those anticipating and recalling the event, brought together dispersed publics with common interactive experience, and was the sociological grounding of a common public life, despite many differences. Such experience is no longer.

This very much applies to Charlottesville. In that city, as racism and white supremacy were asserted, the ways of understanding and opposing these assertions were also publicly performed. There was broad public recognition and response, including shared interactions, but they were fragmented, as much directed between mediated fragments as responding to agreed upon developments. The situation was defined differently depending on how the experience was mediated and with whom, and the understanding of the relationship between the self and the defined situation thus radically differed. In a sense, the situation was not even the same. From right to left there were distinct accounts presented and received. The fragments depended upon their trusted sources of information, as this information was shared by friends on social media.

On the extreme right, there is white supremacy pure and simple, sometimes masked as the defense of heritage or history. There are those who use the mask to tolerate or even support racism and anti-Semitism, including the president of the United States,[6] and those who would distinguish the mask from the issue of heritage. According to *Breitbart*,[7] the violence in Charlottesville is a result of extremists on the left and the right, and largely a consequence of the police not doing their job. Those who condemn the president's response and Steve Bannon's commentary were dismissed as "deplorable conservatives."[8] It is essential, *The Federalist* emphasized, that "white supremacists were not the only thugs tearing up Charlottesville."[9] On these media platforms, the situation is defined, shared and responded to, creating a public set apart from other publics.

On the center right, there is an understanding that conservative principles and the Republican agenda should be distinguished from the extremism of the alt-right. It is divided between those who forcefully condemn the "Unite the Right" demonstration[10] and Trump's response to it, and those who remain relatively silent. This is the zone of established conservatism, taking more or less responsibility for the presence of undisguised blatant racism in American public life. This public fragment does not only depend on Fox and its media friends, though it has important connections to it.

---

6   David Weigel, "In conservative media, an amen chorus defends Trump's comments on Charlottesville violence," *The Washington Post,* August 17, 2017.

7   Ian Mason and Amanda House, "Alt-right activists condemn violence, dispute mainstream account," *Breitbart,* August 13, 2017.

8   Mike Sabo, "A deplorable conservative response to Charlottesville and Bannon," *American Greatness,* August 19, 2017.

9   D. C. McAllister, "White supremacists were not the only thugs tearing up Charlottesville," *The Federalist,* August 14, 2017.

10   John Podhoretz, "Charlottesville proves Trump's doubters right," *New York Post,* August 14, 2017.

It is notable that you, the readers of this chapter and of *Public Seminar*, have not been presented any of these positions. Though we have a broad range of opinion and judgment as a matter of our founding principles, we have not actually been engaging those on the right. Our debates have been left of center.

I am ambivalent about this. On the one hand, principled conservative judgment should be part of any democratic discussion, but on the other hand, an urgency to oppose racism resists such evenhandedness. It is important, even more important, to recognize critically the problem of the enduring legacies of slavery and racism (something rarely found on the right). This is not simply an editorial dilemma, but the result of a fissure in public life, what I have called a bifurcated public sphere[11] as it applies to the global structural transformation of public life.

On the center-left, there is a direct rejection of the blatant racism of the "Unite the Right" demonstration, and a need to rebuke all who apologize for or remain silent about it. This is revealed in all the pieces collected here. There is an understanding that white supremacy is knitted into the fabric of American life, and that a concerted effort needs to be made to oppose raw racism as it appeared in Charlottesville[12] as well as the racism that is institutionalized into normal social practices. One example is the presence of a statue of Robert E. Lee in Emancipation Park, a public park that was once named after the Confederate general. There are differences of opinion about how tight the knitting is,[13] how

11 Jeffrey C. Goldfarb, "The new authoritarianism and the structural transformation of the mediated public sphere I: Reviewing the work of Jürgen Habermas and Hannah Arendt with an assist from Nancy Fraser," *Public Seminar,* August 18, 2017.

12 Melvin Rogers, "White identity and terror in America: Thinking about the events of Charlottesville," *Public Seminar,* August 16, 2017.

13 Michael Weinman, "Charlottesville, Thomas Jefferson, and America's fate: A response

the pattern includes the founders, and about how to unravel it.[14] There is disagreement concerning the link between the foundations of the American polity, and the racism that was present at the founding[15] and ever since. We act and interact in public with these disagreements in mind.

On the left, the link between the foundations of the republic and racism is more commonly recognized, as is the centrality of institutionalized racism, and further, how both developed along with capitalism is a major theme.[16] While for those of the center-left, generally speaking, Charlottesville was a scandal, a stain on the meaning of the ideals of American democracy, those further to the left see Charlottesville as an instantiation of the racism inherent in American democracy, as linked to capitalism. Nothing less than revolutionary change is thus called for. Those "liberals" who don't recognize this are sometimes seen as even more of the problem than those of the alt-right, as was suggested in *Jacobin*.[17]

There is a full range of opinion, but the configuration of the exchange of opinion is divided. That those who took part in the "Unite the Right" demonstration are now included in the general public discussion is the success of the "Unite the Right" social forces.[18] That this hasn't been decisively pushed back presents a

---

to Keval Bhatt," *Public Seminar*, October 22, 2017.

14   Elena Gagovska, "The political landscape post Charlottesville," *Public Seminar*, September 16th, 2017

15   Isaac Ariail Reed, "Jefferson's two bodies: Memory, protest and democracy at the University of Virginia and beyond," *Public Seminar*, October 19, 2017.

16   Nancy Fraser, "From progressive neoliberalism to Trump and beyond," *Public Seminar*, December 21, 2017.

17   Shuja Haider, "One has to take sides," *Jacobin*, August 13, 2017.

18   Jamelle Bouie, "This was a white-power movement showing its strength," *Slate*, August 12, 2017.

major crisis, and it is not just about a shifting balance of power. It challenges democratic politics. Michael Weinman in considering free speech and "Unite the Right,"[19] recently recalled Horkheimer and Adorno's observation that "it is not possible to have a conversation with a fascist. If anyone else speaks, the fascist considers his intervention a brazen interruption. He is not accessible to reason, because for him reason lies in the other person's agreement with his own ideas."

After Charlottesville, this is the profound problem: neo-fascists, Nazis and the KKK are now part of the public debate, even as their opponents hardly see and hear each other and have difficulty coming to a common conclusion about what should be done. Political persuasion is not possible when those with different judgments and positions have little or no contact, and when we pay attention to only those with whom we agree. A significant segment of the population knows about the world through dubious sources. What we expect from news is up for grabs.[20] There is "fake news" as an epithet for serious news reporting, and then there is really fake news.

And we do not only read, listen, and watch different sources of news, information, and opinion, we constitute ourselves as separate and apart, making a political solution to the enduring problems of white supremacy and racism ever more elusive.

We live in separate and decidedly unequal realities in the United States. "If men define situations as real, they are real in their consequences." This is a fundamental principle of interactive sociology, presented in 1928 by William Isaac Thomas and

19 Michael Weinman, "No-platforming, 'Unite the Right,' and new free speech debate," *Public Seminar,* December 26, 2017.

20 Claire Potter, "What do we want from the news?" *Public Seminar,* January 3, 2018.

Dorothy Swaine Thomas. Erving Goffman's dramaturgical sociology is an extensive development of this "Thomas Theorem." The implication of Joshua Meyrowitz's application of Goffman, then, yields what might be called "The Mediated Thomas Theorem": "If people define mediated situations as real, they are real in their consequences." This is where the events of Charlottesville reveal themselves as a crisis in the republic.

The reality of Charlottesville, for the viewers of Fox News, the readers of *Breitbart* and other such platforms supported by social media, has little to do with the reality presented on more reliable sources of news, including MSNBC and CNN, and *The New York Times* and *The Washington Post,* but also *The Wall Street Journal* and *The Economist.*

We are all still in Charlottesville, as we do not share a common definition of our situation, and white supremacy endures. Democratically struggling against the enduring problem, American democracy now requires a fight against the central enduring problems of the mediated (re)public.

Jeffrey C. Goldfarb is the Michael E. Gellert professor of sociology at the New School for Social Research. He is also the publisher of Public Seminar. *His work primarily focuses on the sociology of media, culture, and politics.*

Rachel McKinney

The False Premises of Alt-Right Ideology

Academics Must Understand How the Alt-Right Sees the World if We Are to Resist It

The ethnonationalism typified by Steve Bannon, Richard Spencer, and the alt-right has come home to campus. American universities have seen a surge in intimidation and violence against students of color,[1] a rise in the creation of white power student groups,[2] and the organization of campus speaking tours of alt-right microcelebrities.[3] Academics, then, need to be aware of the contours and function of this ideology: we are on the front lines.

Adequately understanding the alt-right ideology requires us to see how it is different from other strains of racism, how it is different from political frameworks that it might seem superficially similar to, such as Marxist critique, and how it understands and responds to the left's own narratives, frameworks, and discourse. Once we have a grip on the ideology, we can better see its first-order falsehoods, failures, irrationalities, and inconsistencies. This will, hopefully, help us better deal with it in our classrooms and on our campuses, and

---

1 Tasneem Nashrulla, "Here are 28 reported racist and violent incidents after Donald Trump's victory," *Buzzfeed*, November 10, 2016.

2 Lisa Beringer, "When a white supremacist group recruits on campus," *The Progressive*, December 6, 2016.

3 Abigail Edge, "Two nights on Milo Yiannopoulos's campus tour: As offensive as you'd imagine," *The Guardian*, January 28, 2017.

allow our students to see its practitioners as the intellectual charlatans that they are.

An adequate academic response to this ideology will require a proper analysis of its components: the theory of race and gender that it assumes, the theory of political economy it defends, and the political positions it both explicitly and implicitly claims. Jed Purdy has given a very useful overview[4] of two important components of this ideology: its rejection of constitutional constraints, on the one hand, and democratic principles, on the other. Below I say a bit about the theories of gender, race, and political economy the ideology assumes. My discussion here is based on some core documents of neoreactionary thought, including philosopher Nick Land's "Dark Enlightenment" manifesto and the publication of white nationalist Spencer's *Radix Journal*.

The alt-right is ethnonationalist. For ethnonationalists, it is taken as fact that races are natural/biological kinds and that different races have different abilities/talents/dispositions. Appeals to scientific racism, IQ disparity, and "human biodiversity" serve as putative evidence for this claim. Nationality/national identity (American, English, French, etc.) is then taken to be a political manifestation of ethnic/racial/tribal identity. This explains how Muslim and Latinx Americans are not real Americans. The picture claims that just as gender is the "natural manifestation" of sex, nationality is the "natural manifestation" of a race/tribe.

The alt-right is also what we might call heteropatriarchal determinist. For heteropatriarchal determinists, it is taken as fact that "men" and "women" are innate/natural/biological categories; that men and women are dimorphic such that gendered differences in

---

4   Jedediah Purdy, "The anti-democratic worldview of Steve Bannon and Peter Thiel," *Politico Magazine*, November 30, 2016.

characteristions such as behavior *just are* genetically determined differences, that men and women have naturally different abilities/talents/dispositions; and that men and women have different natural roles in sexuality, the gendered division of labor, and family structure.

For the alt-right, social Darwinism/survival of the fittest is true, might makes right, and some form of capitalism is necessary for human prosperity. There is no Lockean proviso. Anarcho-capitalism is therefore legitimate because for any sphere, it is either rational to get yours before someone else gets theirs, or because it is what you "deserve" by ethnonational birthright.

Globally, the economy is a zero sum game between nations/races for the benefits (NB: there are no burdens?) of capitalism (e.g., jobs, wages, wealth, prosperity, welfare/well-being)—i.e., "winners" and "losers." Historically, (white) Americans were winners (in wages, job security, quality of life), but because of negligence and interference by a political class/degeneracy of a culture (see below), (white, male) America is "losing" (see: economic devitalization, deindustrialization, drug addiction, housing crisis, etc.).

The degeneracy story goes something like this. Because capitalism is necessary for human prosperity, owners/bosses are heroes (read: "small businessmen" and "entrepreneurs") rather than villains. However, a global political (not economic) class of elites (elected officials/establishment political parties/lobbyists/overseas allies, aided by media and academia—sometimes this is explicitly racialized as Jewish conspiracy) have materially undermined (through domestic regulation, global trade, and permissive immigration) the ability of the entrepreneurial class to allow wealth and prosperity to "trickle down" to workers via jobs, growth, etc. "Degeneracy" then manifests materially via immigration/migration from Latin America (bringing "drugs" and "rapists," lowering wages), "Islamization," the "contagion" of black violence and poverty, and "dependency" on government assistance.

Academia, the news media, and Hollywood are the cultural arm of this political class. They have aided degeneracy through culture via an ideological program of marginalization and denigration of white identity and masculinity (e.g., the woman-fronted Ghostbusters remake), manipulation/propaganda ("paid protesters"), censorship ("political correctness") and unfair advantage (affirmative action vs. All Lives Matter). This is what the floating signifiers of "political correctness," "safe spaces," "privilege," and "identity politics," are about, and at least partially where the hostility toward movements such as feminism, campus activism, and Black Lives Matter comes from.

The alt-right has a thoroughly individualist and amaterial understanding of oppression. Material conditions of racial and gender oppression (such as segregation, redlining, violence, employment discrimination) are a thing of the past—now, American social institutions are either (a) equal and meritocratic or (b) "rigged" to unfairly favor women and people of color. This explains why ethnonationalists hear words like racism, sexism, misogyny, and privilege as hurt feelings rather than legitimate claims of wrong or harm. Because there are no longer any underlying material conditions that cause or constitute race/gender oppression, critique is all symbolic, a performance of offense and oversensitivity.

This is also why critique against *actually existing* structures like patriarchy and white supremacy is so perversely ineffective here:

it is heard as name-calling/ad hominem, hypocrisy, censorship, emoting, pearl-clutching, and scolding from a class of political elites ostensibly committed to egalitarianism against the words, values, interests, and beliefs of political non-elites (again, sometimes explicitly racialized as an "ethnic minority" of whites).

Despite Donald Trump being elected, American democracy is in crisis. Elections are "rigged" either de facto or *de jure* (e.g., "voter fraud"), voters are too stupid/complacent to make correct choices anyway (either through being "duped" by ideological mechanisms like those above or by inaction/inertia) and "white genocide" means there will be fewer and fewer "real American" voters in the future. So democracy is in crisis. For some this crisis means democracy itself is illegitimate/a failed experiment, and we would be better off with either a benevolent strongman or doing away with federal government altogether (the latter is venture capitalist Peter Thiel's take).

I think it is important to recognize this story for what it is, because it gives us a way of identifying points of vulnerability in the story (e.g., race realism is false, might does not make right, democracy is essential for human freedom, and anarcho-capitalism is a disaster). Our engagement in the classroom and on campus in the age of the alt-right needs to help students foster competing narratives, frameworks, and political alternatives that better describe and explain social reality, and that give students a stake in creating a better world.

Such competing alternative frameworks will include a defense of old-fashioned moral principles like freedom and equality, democratic legitimacy, and the social contract. Also important will be coherent arguments against (anarcho-)capitalism that defend the value of rule-of-law based markets and/or help refocus critique on the economic classes responsible for exploitation, deprivation, and immiseration in the first place—Bernie Sanders's recent town hall in Kenosha county is a good example of what the latter might look like.[5] We can also help our students by refocusing on the structural and material reality of race and gender oppression. Ta-Nehisi Coates's "The Case for Reparations"[6] is a good paradigm for this kind of work.

Finally, we can also model to our students what better political alternatives look like in practice by standing in solidarity with unionizing graduate students[7] and striking staff,[8] by aligning with anti-deportation student and community groups, and by taking a stand in defense of civil liberties like free speech and freedom of association as well as defending the welfare state against forthcoming legislation.

The alt-right has come home to the American campus. Academics must understand how it sees the world if we are to resist it.

Rachel McKinney is a postdoctoral associate in the Humanities Center at the University of Pittsburgh.

5   Jedediah Purdy, "Power and persuasion," *Jacobin*, December 15, 2016.

6   Ta-Nehisi Coates, "The case for reparations," *The Atlantic,* June 2014.

7   Vauhini Vara, "A pioneering union at Columbia," *The New Yorker,* December 5, 2014.

8   Collin P. Poirot, "Harvard workers went on strike and won—here's how they did it and how students helped," *The Nation*, October 27, 2016.

Claire Potter

When the Past Isn't Dead

Slavery's Mark on Higher Education

What does a stained-glass window sound like when it breaks?

It's a soft thud, rather than the sharp crash that you hear when a solid object goes through plate glass. Instead of glass shards crashing to the sidewalk, the lead frames around the colored panes will give way first, causing the window to fold in on itself. Some pieces of glass will hang onto the frame, while others will drop to the ground, some remaining whole if the soft metal around each piece cushions its fall. Like fighting racism in American higher education 70 years after the beginning of the modern civil rights movement, the destruction of stained glass may be initially quick, then slower, resistant, deliberate, incomplete, and frustrating.

In June 2016, Yale University dining hall worker Corey Menafee had recently transferred to a residential college named after South Carolina political theorist and slave owner John C. Calhoun, and he found himself contemplating one of these windows. It was one of about a dozen that depicted a romanticized, prewar American South, installed when Calhoun College was built in the early thirties and picturing slaves picking cotton. An 1804 graduate of Yale College, Calhoun was a prominent politician from South Carolina who devoted his life to radical defenses of white supremacy, states' rights, and chattel slavery. Although he died a decade before the Civil War, Calhoun's theory that majority rule endangered the constitutional rights of the minority provided key legal arguments for the thirteen slaveholding states to secede from the Union in 1861.

What was Corey Menafee thinking about in the few minutes before he destroyed the window on that June morning?

"I just got tired of seeing that image," he told reporter Michelle Chen (*The Nation,* July 26, 2016). "I don't know, something inside me is like, that thing has to come down." Menafee drove the end of his broom through the window. He watched the glass crumple, slightly amazed at his own audacity. As his supervisor screamed at him that he had destroyed private property, Menafee retired to the restroom to prepare for his arrest by shaving and washing up. The police arrived; he was taken down to the central police station on State Street in New Haven, booked, and jailed.

Menafee's action also occurred at the end of a school year in which Yale had been asked to deal with its racial past and its racial present in ways that had not drawn such widespread attention since the eighties, when student protesters demanded that Yale divest from the South African apartheid state. On October 30, 2015, in reply to a university-wide communication asking students to be racially sensitive in their choice of Halloween costumes, Erika Christakis, the associate master of Silliman College, had circulated a response that, some students believed, also called the university's commitment to racial equality into question. Acknowledging that "cultural and personal representation" were difficult issues, she then asked whether there was "no room anymore for a child or young person to be a little bit obnoxious … a little bit inappropriate or provocative or, yes, offensive?" Students of color and their allies exploded in outrage, launching a series of spontaneous and organized demonstrations that led to Christakis and her husband resigning from their administrative roles at the college.

The year of rebellion against racism at Yale that began on Halloween and ended with Menafee's destruction of the window points us to an important fact. Long before white supremacists mustered in Charlottesville, Virginia in late August 2017 to prevent the removal of a Confederate statue near the University of Virginia, the cultural battle over race and memorialization of the Civil War had begun.

Significantly, this was not a southern problem. Yale was one institution of many in the Northeast that was founded, and sustained in its first century, on the profits from human trafficking. In 2003, Ruth Simmons was one of the first college presidents to establish a steering committee on Slavery and Justice at Brown University to research and expose that university's links to the traffic in souls. In response to a report delivered in 2007, among other forms of reparation, Brown affirmed its commitment to an accurate and truthful history of the university; to working with the City of Providence and the State of Rhode Island; to exploring the impact of slavery on the region; and to expanding its commitment to the education of African American people in Providence and elsewhere.

Other colleges and universities had followed suit, but significantly, given the events of the 2015-16 school year, Yale was not one of them. And while the protests turned public attention back to the ugly history of Calhoun's role in championing slavery, Yale President Peter Salovey initially declined to rename the college, citing the importance of not rewriting history.

A few weeks later, Menafee took charge of changing history himself.

The 2017 controversy over removing the statue of Confederate General Robert E. Lee from Emancipation (formerly Lee) Park in

Charlottesville, Virginia, sparked violent protests by organized alt-right groups and counter-protests that included anti-fascist (antifa) elements. It is part of a long history of contested public memorials and an even longer history of the desegregation of higher education in the South. Yet it is only in the last several decades that those conversations have turned northward, allowing us to explain how Menafee found himself in a position to begin the process of ending slavery's grip on one corner of Yale College.

In contrast to the hypervisibility of the Confederate monuments in the thirteen states that seceded from the Union in 1861, many memorials to slaveholding in the states that had united to defeat the Confederacy in 1861, from statues to plaques, are often effectively invisible because they are not a focus for celebration. And these memorials were often not created by Northerners. Tributes to what historian Donald Fehrenbacher has called "the slaveholding republic," Northern Civil War memorials were often bought and paid for by southerners who wanted to ensure that Confederate soldiers and politicians were reintegrated into a national heroic narrative. Among them are the 1891 plaque, recently removed, that was dedicated to Robert E. Lee on the Fort Hamilton military base in Brooklyn, New York; the 1906 cenotaph honoring the Confederate dead in a Madison, Wisconsin cemetery; a 1929 marker near McConnellsburg, Pennsylvania, marking the death of the first Confederate soldier to die on Pennsylvania soil prior to the battle of Gettysburg; and a 2003 memorial to Confederate soldiers who died of disease at a prisoner of war camp in Johnson's Island, Ohio.

While Calhoun College is legally a private space, it quickly became part of the national conversation that questioned why soldiers and politicians who defended slavery ought to be honored. As the conversation about Civil War memory has expanded outward from slavery and the war itself, renaming and removal have become prominent civic activities, particularly on elite campuses where students and faculty of color find themselves in spaces where they are not always fully welcomed. Students at Princeton have demanded that Woodrow Wilson, who segregated Washington D.C., have his name removed from the School of Public and International Affairs; and Harvard University has agreed to remove Columbus Day from its calendar and replace it with Indigenous People's Day.

Similarly, in Northern cities, local governments are beginning to address complaints about questionable historical figures memorialized in public space. On April 17, 2018, the New York City Public Design Commission voted to remove a statue of J. Marion Sims, a physician whose experimental gynecological surgeries were done on enslaved women, from Central Park. In October, Boston—a city at the heart of the nineteenth century abolitionist movement—removed its only Confederate memorial, a tribute to one thousand prisoners of war who died while incarcerated on Georges Island in Boston Harbor.

The conversations that have led to the slow dismantling of monuments to the slaveholders' republic have often emphasized the importance of not disturbing or distorting history. Yet, as many historians have pointed out, the vast majority of these plaques, statues, and named buildings were created for precisely that purpose. Many were installed less than a century ago by the United Daughters of the Confederacy (UDC), an organization that has consistently functioned to rehabilitate the so-called "Lost Cause" of Southern political liberty. Initially founded as a charitable organization to fund the retirement of Confederate veterans and war widows, the UDC quickly expanded its mission to the creation of memorials, the maintenance of Confederate cemeteries, essay competitions, and museums that celebrate the war and the plantation past.

The UDC also has a history of vetting public school textbooks to promote a version of the American past that portrays slavery as a benign institution. "Members of the Daughters looked to the region's past as a means to shape race and gender relations in the New South," historian Carolyn Janney notes in the Virginia Encyclopedia, a task that included the ongoing visual and literary depiction of African Americans in subordinate roles. Such depictions, much like the stained glass windows in Calhoun College, served as both an exemplar for their desired racial present, and as a supposedly harmonious past that was destroyed by government intervention.

Thus, the concerns for history that are often expressed by those who oppose the removal of Confederate memorials ought to be treated with skepticism: they were, and are, a false past intended for a Southern audience and to bolster the political claims of white supremacy. But, as historian David Blight has argued in his 2001 book *Race and Reunion: The Civil War in American Memory,* when the production of these memorials boomed after 1890, northern states also began to accept this false past as part of a process of national reconciliation, one that expanded and institutionalized forms of Jim Crow segregation in all 48 states. As Northerners came to accept segregation, the UDC, which boasted 100,000 members nationwide by World War I, expanded its public memory project, installing statues of Confederate generals like Robert E. Lee and Stonewall Jackson in their communities.

Today, the UDC is like one of the windows in Calhoun College: at a little over 19,000 members, it is a genteel and anachronistic vestige of the slaveholders' republic. By defending memorials to the Confederacy, it perpetuates the numerous humiliations devised to keep emancipated slaves and their descendants in a perpetually subordinate position and reinforces racial inequality. Headquartered in Richmond, less than 70 miles from Emancipation Park in Charlottesville, the organization maintains a robust philanthropy as a 501(c)(3) organization that, by its very nature if not its bylaws, provides scholarships and awards exclusively to young white people.

Currently listed as a neo-Confederate group by the Southern Poverty Law Center, the UDC continues to erect memorials, if more privately, to the Confederate dead. On a recent trip to Decatur, Georgia, I spent a sunny afternoon in a cemetery and found no fewer than a dozen benches, headstones, and cenotaphs that had been erected to honor the Confederate dead since 2000. Yet the privacy of the setting, which encourages personal contemplation, in some ways enhances their power. It is hard not to understand why, nestled among generations of southern dead and decorated with lyrical tributes to sacrifice, the emotions generated among audiences for these memorials sustain the resolve of contemporary white hate groups to preserve and celebrate a Confederate past.

Slavery was not only memorialized at universities, some universities were also sites of enslavement and founded with profits from the slave trade. As a Princeton website explains, the university's "first nine presidents all owned slaves, a slave sale took place on campus in 1766, and enslaved people lived at the president's house until 1822. One professor owned a slave as late as 1840." A Columbia University project, led by historian Eric Foner, reveals that at least half of the university's ten presidents between 1754 and 1865 owned slaves, and that slavery was a "significant feature" of campus life.

Yale's Calhoun College opened in 1933, two centuries after Elihu Yale—who made part of his fortune in the slave trade—gave his original endowment of £800, several crates of books and a portrait of King George I to establish a college to produce ministers for New England. Named long after the heyday of UDC Confederate memorialization, the naming of the college also symbolized how successful that project was in rehabilitating the Lost Cause and Calhoun's reputation at a college that had become a hotbed of abolitionism by the early nineteenth century. Indeed, the naming of the college indicates the suppression of that history: no one who commissioned the set of twelve windows depicting the glories of a plantation past could have seriously imagined that the descendants of slaves would learn, and teach, side by side with the descendants of slaveholders, as they were by 2015.

Indeed, for the first 30 years, Yale enrolled so few students who were not white that the windows may have gone almost unnoticed, except perhaps by the workers of New Haven whose job, like Menafee's, was to clean Calhoun's public spaces.

While African Americans occasionally took degrees from Yale, the desegregation of the university only began in earnest between 1960 and 1970. By 1992, a group of Calhoun College graduating seniors succeeded in persuading the university to post a plaque informing students and visitors of Calhoun's pro-slavery views. A few years later, one of the windows—one that depicted an enslaved man in chains bowing in gratitude to

Calhoun, both standing in the shadow of the Capitol building, was altered: afterwards, the former vice president gazed down benevolently, and mysteriously, on an irregular pane of clear glass. Yet the rest of the windows remained.

African American students and their allies continued to complain, but without result. In fact, Menafee's attention was called to the windows during reunion weekend, when an alumnus who had been active in the movement to remove the windows and rename the college came to a reunion with his ten-year-old daughter. "He was telling us how things used to be when he was an undergrad," Menafee explained to National Public Radio reporter Lynn Neary on July 17, 2016. "And then he mentioned that image was there way back, like, ten years ago when he was there as a student, and he said, It's still there. I mean, you can only imagine the type of emotions that run through an African American, if I can say that, seeing a picture of two slaves—two actual slaves picking cotton."

But to say that Menafee's actions were driven entirely by emotion, or that they were spontaneous, would be wrong: the memorial to Calhoun, to slavery, and to his own subordination under white supremacy had been clarified by this encounter, and it grated on him for days afterwards. Something invisible had suddenly become hypervisible. Menafee thought about the windows for another two weeks, becoming increasingly "tired of looking at that image," as he told Neary. Remembering his decision to destroy a window, Menafee recalled that once he had actually seen the images for what they were, he could not un-see them. "I think it's like Edgar Allen Poe's *The Tell-Tale Heart*," he told her. "It was sitting in the corner of the room ticking away subconsciously—somewhere in my subconscious."

As Menafee punched his broom through the window, the ticking stopped.

Shortly afterwards, Yale removed the remaining windows from Calhoun College dining hall, promising to preserve them in a museum with a proper reference to their origins and meaning. Menafee was fired, but a public outcry, alumni protests, a Change. org petition, fundraising for his legal defense, and student organizing, caused Yale to rehire him. He returned to campus in November 2016, amid a rally organized by the student group called Change the Name. After commissioning an extensive study, chaired by history faculty, in February 2017, Yale announced that Calhoun would become the first Yale College to be named for a woman, Grace Murray Hopper, a pioneering mathematician, computer scientist and rear admiral in the Naval Reserve. Seven months later, one of two new residential colleges would be named for African American civil rights leader Pauli Murray. The other was named for founding father Benjamin Franklin, a slave owner who converted to abolitionism in the 1760s.

Memorials matter, exactly because historical truth matters. Calhoun's slaveocracy may have lost the war, but his theory of the concurrent minority—that imposing the will of the majority is undemocratic—remains a foundational belief for many twenty-first century conservatives who frame political agendas around putative minority status. The belief that human fetuses should be a protected class entitled to civil rights protections; that small groups of conservative students have the right to host speakers that are offensive to the majority of their peers; that opponents of marriage equality should not be forced to serve lesbian and gay patrons; and that Christians have a right to act on faith even when it is against the law, are all examples of ongoing struggles that are partially rooted in Calhoun's political theories, originally devised to defend the traffic in souls.

The past, it is said, is prologue. What happened at Yale in 2016–17 helps us understand the urgency of the struggle at Emancipation Park in Charlottesville less than a year after Menafee returned to his job on Yale's campus. It is a struggle not to erase the past, but to understand it anew; a struggle not to un-see uncomfortable truths about the institutions we value, but to view them unsparingly, and without sentiment.

What does a stained-glass window sound like when it breaks?
It sounds like the future.

Claire Potter is professor of history at The New School and executive editor of Public Seminar. *She is a member of the Yale class of 1980, and donated money for Corey Menafee's legal defense fund.*

Nicholas Baer and Maggie Hennefeld

Prophets of Deceit

Post-Truth Politics and the Future of the Left

> Is foresight commanded by the belief in a prophecy, or safe-guarded through recourse to a historically and philosophically grounded necessity, or perhaps fed from criticism and skepticism?—*Reinhart Koselleck*

> Hindsight, much like the year we're all now desperately looking forward to, is 20/20.—*John Oliver*

The spectacular and traumatic failure of established news sources and polls to predict the outcome of the 2016 presidential election has not only heightened a pervasive sense of uncertainty and anxiety, but also given rise to schizophrenic response patterns in American public discourse. November 9, 2016, inaugurated what many have described as a new era of "liberal panic,"[1] escalating widespread skepticism about the veracity and consequence of all truth-claims and provoking despair over the limited import of reason, critical thinking, and nuanced argumentation about complex issues. Even those who still cling to Enlightenment tenets have regressed to states of paranoid credulity and apocalyptic hysteria, eager to lend credence to unsubstantiated reports, doomsday scenarios, and magical possibilities of escape from national cataclysm.

---

1   Jim Geraghty, "The season of liberal panic," *National Review*, December 27, 2016.

Selected as the Word of the Year 2016,[2] "post-truth" has become the explanatory nomenclature for our political situation, characterized as it is by eroded distinctions between empirical reality and fictional construction, serious journalism and "fake news," and legitimate decisional politics and reality television spectacle. Other commentary has sought to read the "tea leaves" in the form of analogous eras and historical figures or oracular philosophers and schools of thought that ostensibly pointed the way to Donald Trump's presidency. Not unlike the conspiracy theories that circulated after the election, these postmortems should be understood as efforts to make sense of an unfathomable and highly overdetermined historical development through recourse to the concept of fate—a concept, as Georg Simmel wrote, that always entails a "retrospective teleology."

Fatalistic and mythical patterns of thinking were perhaps nowhere more evident than in the ascription of prophetic powers to opinion makers who, like Tiresias, had suggested or predicted the catastrophe to come. While the augurs of national doom ranged from filmmaker Michael Moore to political scholars Allan Lichtman and Helmut Norpoth, we will here consider two disparate public intellectuals whose ideas have gained currency since the election: the late American philosopher Richard Rorty, whose book *Achieving Our Country: Leftist Thought in Twentieth-Century America* (1998)[3] envisioned the rise of a reactionary "strongman," and Russian author and journalist Masha Gessen, whose writings and media appearances have heralded a

2 Oxford Dictionaries, "Post-truth," (2016). Retrieved from https://en.oxforddictionaries.com/word-of-the-year/word-of-the-year-2016.

3 Richard Rorty, *Achieving Our Country: Leftist Thought in Twentieth Century America* (Cambridge: Harvard University Press, 1998), 91.

nihilistic "rock bottom" that can only be countered through hysteric resistance.

What follows are two separate pieces that emerge from our ongoing dialogues about the current impasses of the left, the causes of our "post-truth" situation, and the possibilities for effective resistance. Nicholas Baer restores Rorty's book to its intellectual-historical moment and suggests that despite its remarkable prescience, it has also lost some of its actuality in light of a shifting constellation of postmodernist theory and political action. Maggie Hennefeld then discusses the inheritances of "post-truth" from postmodernism and considers Gessen's call to "be the hysteric"—to conjure the body as text in the absence of more articulate means—in an era marked by the erosion of reason and the freewheeling evacuation of the sign. Rather than providing exhaustive accounts of Rorty's and Gessen's intellectual and political interventions, we will approach the pair as seers who have offered counsel to the left at a time when the limitations and dialectical counterforces of Enlightenment rationalism are blindingly apparent.

NICHOLAS BAER: "POSTMODERNIST PROFESSORS WILL NO LONGER BE CALLING THE SHOTS"

Originally a series of three lectures delivered at Harvard in 1997, Rorty's *Achieving Our Country* addresses issues that would become central to the 2016 election: the globalization of the labor market, the proletarianization of the middle class, increased economic stratification, and frustration with the centrism of the Democratic Party. Although these concerns initially propelled the primary campaign of Bernie Sanders (as well as the earlier Occupy Movement), the broader current of populist anger was ultimately funneled more effectively by

Trump than by Hillary Clinton, who was never able to dispel the image of a middle-of-the-road, "establishment" candidate and career politician. How could the presidency go to a billionaire con man who offered thinly veiled pseudo-solutions to the injustices of American capitalism—or, in Rorty's portentous words, "Why could not the left channel the mounting rage of the newly dispossessed?"[4]

The three abridged paragraphs from Rorty's book that circulated on Twitter and in newspapers around the election drew from Sinclair Lewis's *It Can't Happen Here* (1935) and Edward Luttwak's *The Endangered American Dream* (1993) in prophesying an imminent, Weimar-like era of populist revolt against constitutional democracy:

> [M]embers of labor unions, and unorganized unskilled workers, will sooner or later realize that their government is not even trying to prevent wages from sinking or to prevent jobs from being exported. Around the same time, they will realize that suburban white-collar workers—themselves desperately afraid of being downsized—are not going to let themselves be taxed to provide social benefits for anyone else.
>
> At that point, something will crack. The nonsuburban electorate will decide that the system has failed and start looking around for a strongman to vote for—someone willing to assure them that, once he is elected, the smug bureaucrats, tricky lawyers, overpaid bond salesmen, and postmodernist professors will no longer be calling the shots. . .
>
> One thing that is very likely to happen is that the gains made in the past 40 years by black and brown Americans, and by homo-

---

4   Ibid., 91.

sexuals, will be wiped out. Jocular contempt for women will come back into fashion . . . All the resentment which badly educated Americans feel about having their manners dictated to them by college graduates will find an outlet.[5]

Rorty was undeniably and even uncannily prescient in imagining the rise of a demagogue who would pit himself against an educated elite and political establishment, displacing economic rage against an embattled, negligent government into sadism towards women and racial, religious, and sexual minorities. Notable is Rorty's recognition of the interarticulation of multiple and often-contradictory claims on the part of the "strongman": the Nietzschean self-presentation as both *Übermensch* and emissary of victimized *ressentiment,* the simultaneous advancement of global neoliberalism and nationalist populism, and the paradoxical promise of socioeconomic justice through chauvinist discrimination and systematic disenfranchisement.

The ascription of clairvoyant qualities to Rorty is nonetheless problematic, not least in abstracting the passage from the author's broader argument and intellectual trajectory. The son of Trotskyite socialists and author of the iconoclastic *Philosophy and the Mirror of Nature* (1979), Rorty came to position himself as a (post-)philosopher in the tradition of American pragmatism. If, as Martin Jay notes in *Songs of Experience* (2005), Rorty substituted "the earnest, world-reforming intentions of his predecessors" with "the virtues of private pleasure and the frankly bourgeois liberal ideal of negative freedom,"[6] he squarely returned to

---

5 Ibid., 89–90.

6 Martin Jay, *Songs of Experience: Modern American and European Variations on a Universal Theme* (Oakland: University of California Press, 2005), 302.

political and economic issues in *Achieving Our Country,* where he bemoaned the shift from an active, "reformist left" to a new left characterized by detached spectatorship, self-contempt, and resigned pessimism. Locating this change in the sixties, when American intervention in Vietnam made the United States appear as an irredeemable evil, Rorty argues that it initiated a move from compromise-oriented "real politics" to impatient and utopian cultural radicalism; from a rhetoric of commonality to the fetishism of multicultural difference; from alliance between intellectuals and unions to theoretical obscurantism; and from concrete demands and proposals for economic and legal justice to victim-minded identity politics.

Rorty's critique of the left should be viewed against the backdrop of a fraught intellectual landscape at the close of the past century. In the years prior to *Achieving Our Country,* identity politics had come under critical scrutiny in books as varied as Arthur Schlesinger's *The Disuniting of America* (1991) and Wendy Brown's *States of Injury* (1995), and poststructuralist and postmodernist thought were posited against secular humanism, Habermasian defenses of the project of modernity, and scientific realism (most famously in the Sokal affair of 1996).[7] Moreover, the obtuse language and doctrinal frameworks of "Grand Theory"—or what Rorty had deemed "final vocabulary" in *Contingency, Irony, and Solidarity* (1989)—were targeted for often-polemical attack, precipitating talk of "post-theory" across the humanities. Like Martha Nussbaum in her critique of Judith Butler, "The Professor of Parody" (1999), Rorty was invested in philosophy that engages in piecemeal problem-solving, advancing specific projects for social change in place

---

7   Janny Scott, "Postmodern gravity deconstructed, slyly," *The New York Times,* May 18, 1996.

of abstract, resigned references to hegemony, "the system," or a ubiquitous, inescapable power.

Whatever the merits of such pragmatism,[8] *Achieving Our Country* suffers from hasty generalizations about cultural radicalism and the "apocalyptic French and German philosophy" that, in the author's view, had superseded concern with political economy.[9] Rorty denies the political import of a rather astonishing list of continental philosophers, from Marx and Freud to Lyotard and Jameson. And while reiterating his concurrence with Nietzsche, Heidegger, Foucault, and Derrida in their "criticisms of Enlightenment rationalism," Rorty nonetheless suggests that these thinkers should not be taken up as "guides to political deliberation," but rather "relegated to private life."[10] Against those who espouse cultural pessimism or theorize forms of "impossibility, unreachability, and unrepresentability,"[11] Rorty upholds the doctrines of Walt Whitman and John Dewey, whom he links with the progressive ideal of a classless society as well as a civic religion of exceptionalism, shared social hope, and continued investment in the national project.

Commentators have been troubled by aspects of Rorty's book, especially his call for leftist American patriotism, proscription of religion, and mischaracterizations of Whitman and Dewey. Perhaps most alarming, however, is his reductionist dismissal of other thinkers whose work may lend us critical insight into our own time. To whatever extent Foucault deflated the emancipatory premises of progressivist movements with his conception of modern history in

---

8   Stephen Metcalf, "Richard Rorty's philosophical argument for national pride," *The New Yorker*, January 10, 2017.

9   Rorty, *Achieving Our Country*, 77.

10   Ibid., 96.

11   Ibid., 96.

terms of shifting regimes of power—Rorty writes, "Readers of Foucault often come away believing that no shackles have been broken in the past two hundred years"[12]—the French poststructuralist also changed our entire understanding of issues such as incarceration, mental and sexual pathologization, and neoliberalism and its threat to democratic institutions. It also remains difficult to disregard the writings of Lyotard and Jameson when Trump himself seems to mark postmodernism's *reductio ad absurdum* and to symptomatize the most egregious aspects of multinational capitalism.

Finally, although Rorty takes pains to acknowledge both the blind spots of the reformists and the important contributions of the culturalists, especially with regard to the treatment of women, African Americans, and the LGBTQ community, his narrative remains one of overarching, lapsarian decline. Only from a male, non-minoritarian perspective could the history of the American left appear as a *Verfallsgeschichte* (narrative of decline), with decreasing devotion to the most salient of causes. While Rorty is wary of the "quasi-religious form of spiritual pathos" often deduced from Nietzsche, Heidegger, Foucault, Derrida, and other fellow "antimetaphysical, anti-Cartesian philosophers,"[13] his book itself traces a tacit fall from grace curiously aligned with the very religious notions of "purity" and "sin" that he otherwise criticizes.

The Democratic Party certainly continues to struggle with sustaining a dual commitment to economic equality and social justice, if the recent election cycle is any indication. And even after Barack Obama successfully revived a sense of national hope in the wake of George W. Bush's presidency and amidst the wars in Afghanistan and Iraq, American liberals still face difficulties mobilizing

---

12   Ibid., 7.

13   Ibid., 96.

around a common vision of the country to be realized. Yet much as the increasingly extremist formation of the American right can scarcely be characterized in Rorty's terms—"the right never thinks that anything much needs to be changed: it thinks the country is basically in good shape, and may well have been in better shape in the past"[14]—the key dilemmas of the left have also shifted since the publication of his book two decades ago.

Achieving Our Country appeared at a time when leading strands of thought in the humanities were challenging meta-narratives and absolutist or scientistic conceptions of truth; meaningful sociopolitical gains seemed to hinge on the unsettling of epistemic certainty and the subversion of all normative, universalist validity-claims. A self-appointed representative of "postmodernist bourgeois liberalism" whose work sought to replace experience with language, Rorty was a complex and idiosyncratic figure in this discursive field, dissolving the boundaries between science and literature and insisting that traditional liberal humanism is fully compatible with social construction and with the dismissal of objectivism, moral universalism, and any correspondence theory or ahistorical, transcultural standard of truth. Yet how might his position remain tenable under an administration that lends "deconstruction"[15] sinister new connotations, threatening the livelihood of marginalized subjects and the very future of our planet?

In "Trotsky and the Wild Orchids" (1992), Rorty wrote, "I am often cited by conservative culture warriors as . . . relativistic, irra-

---

14 Ibid., 14.

15 Philip Rucker, "Bannon: Trump administration is in unending battle for 'deconstruction of the administrative state'," *The Washington Post,* February 23, 2017.

tionalist, [and] deconstructing"[16]—adjectives that are now more unequivocally applicable to the right as it pushes anti-foundationalism to its breaking point. Rorty may be correct in questioning the existence of objective values and transcendent truths as well as the possibility of achieving final answers and a synoptic, "God's eye view" (Hilary Putnam). Yet amidst Trump's broadscale attack on local institutions and global structures, on basic civil rights and established scientific consensus, leftists would be ill-advised to emphasize the radical historical contingency of their own moral and political convictions. With the Republican Party propagating "alternative facts" and disavowing even the most incontrovertible forms of knowledge (e.g., on climate change), [17] critics on the left will need to move beyond ironic skepticism and suspicion of the universal, strategically aligning the humanities and natural sciences and buttressing a robust, emphatic conception of truth in the service of social justice and environmental protection.

MAGGIE HENNEFELD: "BE THE HYSTERIC": RESISTANCE IN THE VOID OF MEANING

In a memorable post-election interview on Samantha Bee's satirical *Full Frontal,* Russian author and political dissident Masha Gessen incisively summarizes how Trump "uses language to assert power over reality." Call it "post-truth" babble or simply authoritarian propaganda, "What he is saying is, 'I claim the right to say whatever the hell I please. And what are you gonna do about it?'"

---

16   Richard Rorty, "Trotsky and the Wild Orchids," *Philosophy and Social Hope* (Penguin Books, 1999).

17   Coral Davenport, "E.P.A. chief doubts consensus view of climate change," *The New York Times,* March 9, 2017.

Trump's baffling assertions—which range from alt-facts about voter fraud to paranoid delusions about Obama's wiretapping to blatantly contradictory accusations (such as decrying the "real leaks" of "fake news")—thrive on their very incomprehensibility. The more insane the utterance, the more dangerous the reality of its articulation. As the satirist Andy Borowitz has parodied Trump's auto-referential calamity of logic, "Trump blames bad poll numbers on existence of numerical system."[18] Yet, as Gessen emphasizes, Trump bludgeons language, but he does not mince words. His upending of language from meaning feels just too at home in our culture, in which the cumulative unraveling of moral clarity and epistemological certainty has been under way for quite a long time.

In *Postmodernism, or, the Cultural Logic of Late Capitalism* (1991), Fredric Jameson characterized postmodernism by its crisis-ridden imaginaries: the recurrence of nostalgia and déjà-vu in every sphere of cultural experience—from media aesthetics to public spaces to commercial architecture. Postmodernism gives aesthetic form to the rampant social and economic crises of the deregulated neoliberal state. In other words, the postmodern tyranny of the empty signifier—playfully stylized through a proliferation of irony, pastiche, and nostalgia—symbolizes the erosion of democracy's social and civic institutions and its volatile financial markets. As Arjun Appadurai puts it in *Modernity at Large*, "All this is par for the course, if you follow Jean Baudrillard or Jean-François Lyotard into a world of signs wholly unmoored from their social signifiers (all the world's a Disneyland)…a synchronic warehouse of cultural scenarios, a kind of temporal central casting, to which recourse can be taken as appropriate."[19]

---

18 Andy Borowitz, "Trump blames bad poll numbers on existence of numerical system," *The New Yorker,* August 15, 2016.

19 Arjun Appadurai, *Modernity at Large* (Minneapolis: University of Minnesota Press, 1996), 30-31.

Postmodernism's empire of decentered signs has always risked walking the plank into the void of non-meaning, wherein any truth can be desacralized, any moral conviction co-opted, and any social or environmental crisis relativized. Such pervasive anxiety about losing our grip on meaning and reality now feels tediously familiar, though the stakes of slipping too far along the signifying chain have reached an alarming threshold. When "truth bombs" can signify a greater violence than anti-jihadist drone attacks, how do we navigate the actual effects and dangerous consequences of a regime so aptly filtered through surrealist humor and absurdist parody? Trump's presidency has already been declared Dadaesque performance art,[20] a voter-sourced analog to the Cold War-period television spy series *The Americans,* a dystopian punishment for the hegemony of reality television, and a source text for the return of Ubu Roi (as "Ubu Trump")[21]: Alfred Jarry's outrageous 1896 play about a grotesque king that inspired the rise of modernist movements including surrealism, Dadaism, and the theater of the absurd.

For all the violence that Trump's outbursts inflict upon language, they are shadowed by concrete actions that provoke a very different register of disbelief: the absurdity of post-truth nonsense corroborates the monstrosity of unlawful governance. Trump's performative utterances of his paragon pro-Semitism echo his policy endorsements of an Israel-Palestine one-state solution, while his puzzling declarations of his visible anti-racism hang heavy against the horrendous surge in hate crimes since his election. ("Number one, I'm the least anti-Semitic person you've ever seen

---

20 Erik Vance, "Donald Trump is the world's greatest performance artist," *The Last Word on Nothing,* September 22, 2014.

21 Isaac Ariail Reed, "Trump as Ubu Roi: On the charismatic appeal of vulgarity," *Public Seminar,* June 6, 2017.

in your entire life. Number two, racism, the least racist person.")[22]

The problem, evidently, is that Trump's executive theater of the absurd evokes a mode of disbelief incompatible with that of his authoritarian lawlessness: preposterous laughter versus civil resistance. Can the laughing spectator of Stephen Colbert's "It's Funny Because It's Treason"[23] also be the body on the front line when Trumpism runs roughshod over American civil liberties and democratic institutions—deporting immigrants and refugees, suppressing enfranchisement, privatizing state agencies, undermining the rule of law, and repealing anti-discrimination and environmental protections?

Since the election, the hashtag #NothingMatters has gone viral in tandem with Gessen's own rising celebrity as a poster child for the oppositional powers of political nihilism: the suspicion that liberal humanist values and codification of equal rights are themselves something of a farce. A refugee from Vladimir Putin's autocratic state and author of the scathing biography *The Man Without a Face: The Unlikely Rise of Vladimir Putin* (2012), Gessen's wisdom oscillates between justified cynicism and impassioned resistance. Her bestselling book about the Russian feminist punk rock protest band, *Words Will Break Cement: The Passion of Pussy Riot* (2014), looks to the powers of spectacular disruption, guerilla street protest, and feminist LGBTQ civil activism to unseat the false thrones of populist autocracy. Like Rorty's *Achieving Our Country,* Gessen's "Autocracy: Rules for Survival"[24] (which include taking the

---

22 Eli Watkins, "Trump tells Jewish magazine's reporter to 'sit down,' blames anti-Semitism on 'the other side,'" *CNN,* February 16, 2017.

23 The Late Show with Stephen Colbert, "Michael Flynn's White House tenure: It's funny 'cause it's treason," *The Late Show with Stephen Colbert* via YouTube, 15 February, 2017.

24 Masha Gessen, "Autocracy: Rules for survival," *The New York Review of Books,* November 10, 2016.

autocrat at his word, no matter how unbelievable his claims, and remaining alarmed and outraged despite small signs of normality) has been frequently cited and widely shared on social media since the election.

As Gessen advises Samantha Bee's laughing feminist spectator on *Full Frontal,* "The thing we can do [to subvert autocracy] . . . is actually to continue panicking. Continue to be the hysteric in the room," Bee interrupts, laughing, "I can stay hysterical!" Gessen: "Just continue panicking, write a note to yourself of what you would never do, and when you come to the line, don't cross it."

Gessen's feminist call for mass-hysterical panic feels all too proportionate in this cultural climate, in which misogyny and homophobia have been casually emboldened while anti-discrimination laws are incrementally eroded. The mass psychology of this collective loss of rights follows a familiar script. *Teen Vogue* recently warned its readers that "Donald Trump Is Gaslighting America,"[25] invoking the 1944 Hollywood film (adapted from a British play) about a husband who sadistically manipulates his wife into believing that she is going insane. When the disbelief provoked by Trumpist rhetoric is rivaled only by a looming despair about the potential for any effective resistance, perhaps hysteria is more than an energizing metaphor, but a new frontier for understanding the somatic and environmental stakes of social discourse and political language.

This is what hysteria does at its core: it somaticizes language against the impossibility of self-expression and symbolic articulation. Nineteenth-century female hysterics converted fruitless protest into corporeal spectacle. Their astonishing symptoms included

---

25   Lauren Duca, "Donald Trump is gaslighting America," *Teen Vogue,* December 10, 2016.

somnambulism, phantom paralysis, uncontrollable barking and tongue-clacking, epilepsy, fugue states, double-vision, unending mirthless laughter, and cartoonish bodily flexibility (such as the performance of unreal acrobatic poses that the French neurologist Jean-Martin Charcot aptly classified as *clownisme*). Female hysterics were ostensibly repressed women who accessed their own bodies as expressive texts in the absence of more rational or expedient means of communication.

Coming from the Greek word *hystera,* meaning uterus, hysteria is of course a notoriously gendered malady: a condition that primarily afflicted bereaved widows in ancient Greece, whereby the womb becomes dislodged due to inactivity and starts wandering around the body, giving rise to a legion of physically baffling symptoms. Though modern clinicians (such as Charcot, Janet, Breuer, and Freud) insisted on de-essentializing hysteria, approaching the ailment as psychosomatic rather than organic, its gendered connotations are inescapable.

What, then, does it mean to "be the hysteric" in the twenty-first century context of "post-truth," "alt-fact," "fake news," #Nothing-Matters-era Trumpism? At face value, the metaphor of hysteria provides a springboard for refusing to accept debilitating social losses as gradually normal (i.e., "to normalize"), even when the previous baseline for normality already left plenty of cause for disenchantment and cynicism. The hysteric's body is a stage for the return of repressed or marginalized truths: the necessity of asserting one's voice when confronted with the unmooring of any linguistic discourse or signifying system that might foster and sustain it.

Like hysteria, Trumpism, with its exuberant address[26] to instinct above reason, relies on the urgency of irrational modes of think-

---

26   Michael Weinman, "Tyrant, demagogue, or fascist: Which archetype fits President Trump?" *Public Seminar,* February 19, 2017.

ing and communication. Following many autocrats, Trump has branded himself the voice of truth against political dishonesty—better to lie in plain sight than to deceive or condescend. Gessen, in a recent *New York Times* piece, "In Praise of Hypocrisy,"[27] (February 18, 2017) reflects on this paradox of sincere untruth by invoking Hannah Arendt's *The Origins of Totalitarianism*. She writes: "Fascists the world over have gained popularity by calling forth the idea that the world is rotten to the core... Arendt described how fascism invites people to 'throw off the mask of hypocrisy' and adopt the worldview that there is no right and wrong, only winners and losers." Trump may lie through his teeth, but, to his supporters, it feels less dishonest because he does so out in the open.

This amplified earpiece for brazen discourse, which Trump has exploited, is part and parcel of what the *Economist* has described as *dégagisme:* "A popular urge to hurl out any leader tainted by elected office, establishment politics or insider privilege"[28] (upcoming European elections loom large, with populist candidates such as Marine Le Pen, Frauke Petry, and Beppe Grillo riding the wave of plain-spoken, anti-establishment, nostalgically nationalist sentiment). The maxim "Take Trump seriously, not literally" reveals a belief in his words that exceeds conscious reason, appealing directly to emotional instinct and corporeal sensation.

His cries of "Lock her up!," "Build a wall!," and "Make America Great Again!"—which range from illegal, to unfeasible, to inscrutable—solicit overwhelming visceral responses from the bodies of his exultant supporters. As Jacqueline Rose has noted,

---

27 Masha Gessen, "In praise of hypocrisy," *The New York Times,* February 18, 2017.

28 "The urge to elect an insurgent is helping Marine le Pen and Emmanuel Macron in France," *The Economist,* February 16, 2017.

Trump's election "licensed the obscenity of the unconscious."[29] It is precisely the jouissance of these hysterical chants that makes their targets (women, LGBTQ folks, immigrants, people of color) feel so vulnerable and at risk in Trump's America. More than a symptom of *dégagisme,* this tyranny of unreason provides a long-awaited remedy to the alienation, fatigue, and nostalgia of postmodern late capitalism, wherein signifiers slip willy-nilly from their meanings and referents. The false promises of neo-liberal corporatism and global multiculturalism have produced not social revolution (at least not yet) but wistful regression—to an earlier time when economic prosperity was guilelessly structured around the racial hierarchies of white supremacy.

Pundits struggle to assert the most apt historical analogy to predict and contextualize the political events that are currently unfolding. Is America today that of Putin's Russia circa 2000, or Erdoğan's Turkey circa 2002, or perhaps Netanyahu's Israel circa 2009? More ominously, are we hurtling towards Sinclair Lewis's *It Can't Happen Here:* an alt-history of 1935 fascist America under the populist President Buzz Windrip? If so, then what recourse remains to avert the fact of retrospective disaster? Could it still be 1933 (before the Reichstag Fire and Hitler's militarization of the Rhineland) or is it already 1939? Somewhere between traumatic recurrence and bad déjà-vu, Trumpism's throwback to mid-twentieth century fascism (now under the auspices of runaway neoliberalism) represents both yet another cultural scenario "in the synchronic warehouse" of postmodernism's global playground and radically uncharted territory that is overwhelming cause for mass alarm and passionate opposition.

---

29   Jacqueline Rose, "Donald Trump's victory is a disaster for modern masculinity," *The Guardian,* November 15, 2016.

Against the spread of Nazism in forties Europe, the German émi-gré filmmaker Ernst Lubitsch put a comedic spin on Hamlet's existential soliloquy. Lubitsch's controversial 1942 Hollywood film *To Be or Not to Be* depicts a farcical troupe of Polish actors who must impersonate Hitler and other Nazi officials to save the world from the ravages of Nazi barbarism. The double entendre of Lubitsch's film title refers to the simultaneity of playing a role and continuing to survive. Gessen has offered a gendered but timely revision of fascism's theatrical double bind (could there have been Auschwitz without first the brown shirts and black boots?): *to be the hysteric or not to be the hysteric?* Is that even a question? Hysteria, by definition, misses the point of ontology—it is the somatic recourse of the linguistically dispossessed.

In this vein, Gessen has cautioned against shiny objects à la anti-Ruskie conspiracy narratives, wherein paranoia about Manchurian subterfuge and sensationalist treason serves as an easy "crutch for the American imagination . . . to explain how Trump could have happened to us."[30] But there are dangers to Gessen's undying nihilism. By dismissing all seductive explanations as "conspiracy traps," we risk romanticizing hysteria as somehow purified of ideological deception or political calculation. As long as "kompromat" and "Russiagate" do not quell our hunger for action and mobilization, it is wrong to read them as mere cognitive foils for repeating the old refrain: "It can't happen here."

Victorian hysteria parlayed paranoid neurosis into spectacular protest. As a postmodern gesture, perhaps it will similarly substantiate the pervasive crisis of truth and reason within cultural discourse. Whether righteous resistance or yet another sign in the void, the

---

30   Masha Gessen, "Russia: The conspiracy trap," *The New York Review of Books,*
March 6, 2017.

bodily theater of anti-authoritarian panic—refusing to accept as normal what's beyond the line of one's moral conviction, and then laying one's body on the line to stave off the dangerous slippages of political relativism—may just be our very key to salvation.

Nicholas Baer is collegiate assistant professor and Harper-Schmidt Fellow at the University of Chicago. Maggie Hennefeld is an assistant professor of cultural studies and comparative literature at the University of Minnesota.

Melvin Rogers

White Supremacy, Fear and the Crises of Legitimation

Reflections on the Mistrial in the Murder Case of
Walter Scott and the Election of Donald Trump

I

For many of us, December 5, 2016, was a jarring day. Circuit Court Judge Clifton Newman declared a mistrial in the murder case of Walter Scott. That the jury could deadlock was surprising. Many of us recall the video of former South Carolina police officer Michael Slager, who is white, firing a barrage of bullets in the back of the fleeing Scott, an African American man. The decision underscored once more the categorically unequal status that nonwhites, especially African Americans, occupy—an inequality that fueled a series of major protests in cities across this country, beginning in 2014, and propelled the Black Lives Matter network to national recognition.

We are, however, likely to miss the importance of this decision if we do not connect it to another jarring day: November 9, 2016. Many of us woke up—some of us never slept—to the announcement that Donald Trump would be the forty-fifth president of the United States. Given that Trump's campaign was fueled by racism, xenophobia, and concern for the economic precarity of white Americans in particular, and that it received the support of white nationalists, it seemed surprising that Trump secured the presidency. Not because Americans necessarily believed those dimensions of our cultural and polit-ical life had died—rather, because we believed that those fea-tures were insufficiently robust and organized to secure Trump the presidency. Yes, we all know the data is complicated, but we would be hard pressed to deny that for those who voted for Trump, his political vision of racist exclusion and domination was not enough to disqualify him from the presidency. Van Jones's now famous remark on CNN regarding Trump's historic win still seems appropriate more than a month later: "This was a whitelash against a changing country."

These two seemingly disparate moments—Slager's mistrial and Trump's win—both call into question the legitimacy of the politi-cal and legal institutions that define the American polity. The first crisis of legitimacy relates to categorical insecurity, while the sec-ond is tied to the presumption of power by white Americans, which was perceived to be under assault, leading to the reactionary poli-tics that produced Trump. But the two legitimation crises are not of the same character and, in fact, are at cross-purposes with each other, generating an impasse that is not readily overcome.

II

In the wake of similar high-profile police shootings where wrongdoing seems so clear, but goes unpunished, the Slager trial crystallizes what many believe—that police officers can kill black Americans with impunity. The greatest obstacle to freedom and equality thus appears to be a society in which citizens are habituated to recognize some among themselves as worthy of care, concern, and justice, while believing they can withhold these important moral goods from others. Black Americans thus find themselves living in a society in which they are asked to follow the law, and yet, are simultaneously unprotected by political and legal institutions. The direction of loyalty goes from black Americans to the state, but not the other way.

This condition is the quintessential expression of a legitimation crisis—what philosopher Jürgen Habermas described in 1973 as an inability of the state to secure, institutionally and morally, the goods for which it was established, thus destroying any faith the citizenry would otherwise place in its institutions. The ascendancy of Black Lives Matter is not merely the result of trying to properly align one aspect of American society—in this case, the criminal justice system—to the appropriate values that define our political and social life. Rather, the movement is a claim that the way we order our collective lives and dispense justice benefits only one group.

And yet, the Trump victory makes clear that a sizeable segment of the population rejects an American future that is more diverse, more inclusive, and potentially more equal. It rejects, in other words, precisely the vision to which Black Lives Matter gave expression. The "whitelash" to which Jones points should be read as an attempt by white Americans to address what they too perceive as a legitimation crisis: they can no longer trust their racial identity to secure for them the entitlements (including economic ones) that it previously had.

Both of these crises of legitimacy are fueled by the workings of white supremacy, but they are in obvious and inescapable conflict. The first crisis—namely, that nonwhite lives are valued less than white lives—cannot be addressed without intensifying the second. And addressing the second, as through the ascendancy of Trump, involves doubling down on the politics of domination and arbitrary violence that generate the first.

III

When we treat white supremacy as the operating logic that ties these two moments together, we are faced inexorably with white supremacy's other operating feature—namely, fear. In police shootings of unarmed black people, the police officer is often found saying that he "feared for his life," or in the case of Slager, felt "total fear." White supremacy creates a condition wherein the "natural" or "normal" status of black people easily mingles with traits of criminality in the minds of observing citizens, conditioning their behavior toward black people, regardless of any observable nonthreatening conduct on display. After all, in the case of Michael Scott, he was running away. White supremacy thus creates a social epistemic context that renders the status of blacks—the lives they lead and the activities they undertake—uncertain, subject to arbitrary domination at best and death at worst.

But such dangers are unable to come into view precisely because of the normalization and legitimation of the claims of fear often provided by police officers specifically, and white Americans generally. Just as the logic of white supremacy involves valuing white lives more than others, it leads to the presumption that white Americans are (a) accurate when they describe the context in which they engage nonwhites as threatening and (b) are therefore legitimate in their use of force to extinguish the source of fear. This is because the security of white lives is to be affirmed at all costs, even when it renders nonwhite lives disposable. Black Americans are not unique in suffering as a result of this logic, even if they are the most obvious victims of it.

This leads to a deeper problem. The avoidance of a legitimation crisis for white Americans not only involves legal and political institutions channeling the supremacy of whiteness, but also protecting whites from the existential fear that is the hallmark of nonwhite lives. This involves a constitutive distortion of democracy. As John Dewey made clear in his 1927 work, *The Public and its Problems,* democracy involves treating public life as an open sphere—a network across which problems and concerns get communicated by different groups seeking relief, and in our coordinated effort to address such concerns, we build a shared life together founded on the principle of equal regard. In contrast, white supremacy involves a distortion of democracy by treating the concerns of white Americans as the true and legitimate concerns of the polity and therefore the only concerns in need of redress. If democracy opens the space of power by preventing any one group from claiming exclusive authority to use it, white supremacy renders public life static by tethering it to whiteness. The result is to render the concerns of nonwhites as either of less importance or unworthy of any consideration if such consideration involves a diminution of whiteness. This is something about which African Americans have long been aware, from the nineteenth century to the present, even as they debated whether to see this distortion as partial or total.

But we know that black Americans are not unique in suffering as a result of this logic if we focus on Trump's campaign for the presidency. "Make America Great Again," the mantra of his campaign, was consistently wedded to the proposition that America is no longer great because "illegal" immigrants are stealing jobs from white people—largely white men—because Muslim-Americans are threatening to supplant the values of American democracy, and because America is in danger of being effeminized by both the disabled and the LGBTQ community. Similar to the treatment of black Americans, Trump demonized or pathologized all other groups. As Charles Blow rightly observed in August 2016:

"'Make America Great Again' is in fact an inverted admission of loss—lost primacy, lost privilege, lost prestige." But these losses take on the force that they do because they generate the perception of uncertainty regarding one's status, and, correspondingly, fear of falling to a level that would make white Americans merely equal to their nonwhite counterparts.

The legitimation crisis for white Americans is thus a legitimation crisis of whiteness and the security their identity otherwise provided them. And yet, it is precisely the institutionalization of whiteness that various groups such as African Americans often see as the culprit for their ill treatment. But herein lies the rub: who among us would readily give up such security, even for the noble values of equality, freedom, and justice? The troubling issue that we must grapple with is the possibility that white supremacy generates far too many psychological, libidinal, cultural, political, and economic goods to be sufficiently destabilized or decentered. And the goods, although not few in number, that seemingly come from a racially inclusive society that affirm the equal dignity of persons appear far too weak to create an ethical society that can find institutional and cultural support. Overcoming this impasse suggests, at a minimum, that tinkering within the existing structures of the United States or imagining that those structures would permit a radical transformation of values would simply not match the gravity of the problem.

Melvin Rogers is an associate professor of political science at Brown University. He is the author of The Undiscovered Dewey: Religion, Morality, and the Ethos of Democracy *and the forthcoming* The Darkened Light of Faith: Race, Democracy, and Freedom in African American Political Thought.

Neil Roberts

Authoritarianism and Civilization

Du Bois, Davis, and Trump

In 1890 the young W. E. B. Du Bois delivered the Harvard University Commencement address "Jefferson Davis as a Representative of Civilization."[1] Du Bois focused on a central figure of nineteenth-century America as he prophesied the meanings of freedom, democracy, and what American life—or more accurately, civilization—would look like over the next hundred years and beyond for the white world, the black world, and other nonwhite populations that hitherto occupied spaces outside the epicenters of civil and political society.

Born in Kentucky, Davis held the offices of U.S. representative and senator for the state of Mississippi and later secretary of war under President Franklin Pierce.[2] Following Pierce's failure at the 1856 Democratic National Convention to acquire presidential renomination support from party delegates, Davis ran again, won, and went back to Congress as a senator. Yet with the 1860 election of Abraham Lincoln and escalating distrust between South and North, Davis resigned his Senate post.

After ensuing Southern secession, Davis assumed the presidency of the Confederate States of America, maintaining the position until the Civil War's end. Davis had poor health much of his adult-

---

1   W. E. B. Du Bois, "Jefferson Davis as a representative of civilization, June 1980,"
W. E. B. Du Bois Papers (MS 312). Special Collections and University Archives, University of Massachusetts Amherst Libraries.

2   Jefferson Davis, "The papers of Jefferson Davis," Rice University.

hood and detractors internal to the Confederacy. While underestimated by peers and despised by several prominent Confederate politicians and generals, he nevertheless forged an obedient coalition and crafted a resolute model of governance and rule. Although Davis lived until the post-Reconstruction year before Du Bois's speech, his thoughts and actions as Confederacy president provided core teachable moments.

Du Bois considers Davis a person whose self-conception is that of "a typical Teutonic hero" and whose notion of leadership personifies "the idea of the Strong Man." By Strong Man, Du Bois means a leader espousing "[i]ndividualism coupled with the rule of might." The Strong Man, suffuse with strength, privileges the "I" and self-assertion over the "Thou." The Strong Man bolsters civilization through "stalwart manhood and heroic character" on the one hand and "moral obtuseness and refined brutality" on the other. The Strong Man often relies on disgruntled and violent mobs, adherents who are, as Hannah Arendt observes, angry masses that feel excluded from previously accessed corridors of politics, believe their standing in society has evaporated compared to the prior generation, loathe heterogeneous society as is, and cry out for the homogeneous order the Strong Man promises.[3] The Strong Man's patriarchal idea of civilization is intimately tied to racial orders, and it is his vision of a future world that augurs the consolidation and regeneration of the white race above all other races.

Du Bois contrasts the Strong Man with the Submissive Man, characterized by weakness, a commitment to truth, and desire to acquiesce to the Thou, the You, the part of personhood not obsessed with the image of the being reflected back in the mirror. Whereas the American Teuton, of which Davis is exemplary, is indicative of

---

3   Hannah Arendt, *The Origins of Totalitarianism* (New York: Harcourt, Brace & World, 1966).

the Strong Man, the Negro is for Du Bois the archetypal Submissive Man that Davis dismisses.

Ironically, the Strong Man and the Submissive Man need one another, their diametrically opposed views notwithstanding. Otherwise, the polity they inhabit devolves into despotism or slavery, and not merely for those emboldened at any given time with the might and right of state.

Davis, "the peculiar champion of a people fighting to be free in order that another people should not be free," missed the inseparability of the I and the You. He refused to admit the ways we're interconnected, in relation, despite our pluralistic and differential conceptions of the free life and in spite of attempts by agents of state and their lackeys to interfere, dominate, segregate, deport, and annihilate.

Davis's Strong Man hubris spawned a vitriolic, angry, white nationalist, revolting mass. It also led to his downfall, the Confederacy's decline, and that of American civilization as he conceived it, in large measure due not only to abolitionists but also the actions of fugitives and slave agents catalyzing its genesis. It didn't, however, obliterate the wages of whiteness and political philosophy of white supremacy in the post-1865 polity. Du Bois documents this in *The Philadelphia Negro, The Souls of Black Folk,* and, most notably, *Black Reconstruction in America,* as do scholars such as C. L. R. James, Frantz Fanon, Annette Gordon-Reed, and Nell Painter. This last point haunts us today.

Authority and authoritarianism undergird Du Bois's prognostications. An agent with "authority" demands dogged obedience, compliance, and that the urges toward ressentiment by the subjects of sovereign command are dispelled. "Authoritarianism" is the structural macropolitical systemization of a type of statecraft designed by what Theodor Adorno and collaborators call an authoritarian personality.[4] It is a hierarchical social, political, and economic order militating against egalitarianism. Moreover, as Arendt notes in "What Is Authority?," we shouldn't confuse authoritarianism with tyranny, for "the tyrant rules in accordance with his own will and interest, whereas even the most draconian authoritarian government is bound by laws."[5]

Du Bois wrestles with Davis's legacy because Davis oversaw a confederation based on slavery and apparatuses of unfreedom enshrined in jurisprudence. Du Bois cautions against ambivalence, nihilism, and avoidance of the afterlife of chattel slavery, first since modes of enslavement sanctioned by law mutated and have been upheld at different junctures by authoritarian personalities, though not always in the public sphere by the prime executive. An amplification of these chilling effects occurs when the entity wielding authority—whose public beliefs defend racism, sexism, xenophobia, chauvinism, and rabid masculinity—is commander-in-chief. Second, struggle, resistance, and abolitionist challenges to authority and authoritarianism are as much a tradition as the tradition their actions seek to dislodge. Never forget that.

Our current moment is unprecedented. Yet past lessons offer signposts for future judgments and decision-making. President-elect Donald Trump entered his 2016 campaign a noted businessman, consummate reality TV performer, and a political chameleon. In the process of winning the Republican primary and shockingly defeating Hillary Clinton, Trump clarified certain issues and left many policy positions open-ended.

---

4   T. W. Adorno, Else Frenkel-Brunswik, Daniel J. Levinson, and R. Nevitt Sanford, "The authoritarian personality," *Studies in Prejudice Series*, Volume 1, 1950.

5   Hannah Arendt, *Between Past and Future* (New York: Penguin Books, 2006).

What's incontrovertible is Trump's authoritarian personality.[6] Only time will tell what type of authoritarian president Trump will be, whether Davis reincarnated or otherwise. And if his senior administrative appointments are any indication, particularly the ghastly selection of avowed white nationalist Stephen Bannon as top White House advisor, then we'd be foolish to assume Trump's stated public beliefs and campaign promises are one big bluff. *Parrhesia* is hard to digest.

We have a choice in the Age of Trump: ignore history and our intrinsic abilities for action, thereby reifying the authoritarian order Trump very much plans to implement. *Or* protest. Petition. Resist authoritarianism and its mob enforcers. Organize. Unlock our political imaginations. Believe firmly our actions can match our convictions.

"American democracy" is an unrealized and perhaps unrealizable Platonic ideal, but democracy in America, in the hemisphere, and in the globe, measured in nodes of progress, is attainable. Progress, as with regress, comes in stages. And like freedom, the theory of relativity, and quantum mechanics, the meaning of progress and attendant strivings for it begin with acknowledging a foundational phenomenon: perpetual flight.

Flight operates betwixt, between, and beyond the options of Strong Man and Submissive Man. "Human" progress, a consequence of ongoing marronage, beckons us.[7]

Neil Roberts is associate professor of Africana studies, political theory, and the philosophy of religion at Williams College. His book Freedom as Marronage *is the recipient of many awards. He is president of the Caribbean Philosophical Association.*

---

6   Neil Roberts, "No-rule: Thinking about Obama vs. Trump through Hannah Arendt and C. L. R. James," *Public Seminar*, August 4, 2016.

7   Neil Roberts, *Freedom as Marronage* (Chicago: University of Chicago Press Books, 2015).

Michael Sasha King

Sitting to Stand

Protest, Patriotism, and the Endurance of
White Supremacy

In his *New York Times* op-ed, "The Uses of Patriotism," [1] David Brooks chides high school football players who would protest racism by not standing for the national anthem. Invoking American Studies pioneer Perry Miller, Brooks argues that patriotic self-criticism and radical hope, not abstention, are the foundation of American values. Through these partnered ideas, he claims, the United States fuses into a nation. Thus, it is the duty of all Americans to participate in patriotic rituals because they bind us into a nation. Brooks is not alone in his critique.

Since San Francisco 49ers quarterback Colin Kaepernick decided to stay seated[2] during the national anthem, this country has witnessed an extended attempt to diminish his act. Former quarterback Boomer Esiason[3] said that Kaepernick was "about as disrespectful as any athlete has ever been," whereas Hall of Fame baseball manager Tony La Russa called Kaepernick's sincerity into question. Fox News correspondent Bill O'Reilly went even further, arguing that "no nation is perfect,"[4] but the presence of racial injustice described by Kaepernick

---

1   David Brooks, "The uses of patriotism," *The New York Times*, September 16, 2016.

2   Mark Sandritter, "A timeline of Colin Kaepernick's national anthem protest and the athletes who joined him," *SB Nation*, September 25, 2017.

3   Bob Glauber, "Colin Kaepernick draws criticism from Boomer Esiason, praise from Bart Scott," *Newsday*, August 30, 2016.

4   Erik Wemple, "Fox News's Bill O'Reilly leverages Kaepernick social-justice debate for book sales," *The Washington Post*, September 15, 2016.

and others is grossly overstated. Most recently, Supreme Court Justice Ruth Bader Ginsburg surprised some and confirmed for others that even the most stalwart proponents of justice can be and often are insufficiently critical on matters of race when she told Katie Couric that Kaepernick's decision not to stand was "dumb and disrespectful"[5] (Ginsburg has since apologized). Like Brooks, these four understand patriotism to be bigger than any individual or race.

They are right that recent protests transcend any single event or person. They are wrong, however, that patriotic rituals form a binding phenomenon that exceeds questions of racism. To the contrary, the continued presence of racism within the United States severs our national connection and, in doing so, renders acts of uncritical patriotism a mockery of the American polity. What good, we might ask, are rituals when they require one to forego national reckoning for feel-good acquiescence? When approached from this vantage, sitting or taking a knee becomes less a gesture of disrespect than a demand for the kind of critical analysis Brooks and others understand to be the crucial element of American hope. It is an invitation for Americans to interrogate white supremacy in all its shifting and often complicated manifestations.

For many, the invocation of white supremacy conjures violent events and abhorrent laws from the past. However, these historical facts are better thought of as consequences of white supremacy, not the enduring and wily thing itself. At base, white supremacy is nothing more than the institutional empowerment of white desire over and above the rights, protections, and needs of citizens of color. It is not a specific set of laws or rules that exist historically,

5   Nick Wagoner, "Ruth Bader Ginsburg says national anthem protests are 'really dumb,'" *ESPN*, October 10, 2016.

but rather a network of legal, social, and moral responses that privilege white interests. White supremacy exceeds specific laws, which are always historical responses to particular desires.

Much like the radical hope Brooks cites, white supremacy has existed throughout this nation's history. The Constitution includes a clause that postponed all efforts to prohibit the importation of enslaved Africans for twenty years. Largely a compromise meant to appease delegates in Georgia and South Carolina, the clause placed the interests of white slave owners above the protection and interests of enslaved Africans. Nearly 80 years later, state legislatures in the South installed Jim Crow laws, sanctioning white desire for segregation. In the North, practices such as redlining had a similar effect. In each case, white desire superseded the rights and protections of black people.

White supremacy is not limited to oppressive sanctions and events. It also exists within acts we consider liberating. One of the more famous examples is the Supreme Court's 1954 decision of *Brown v. Board of Education,* which desegregated public schools and effectively overturned the court's 1896 "separate but equal" doctrine. Though this decision is often presented as a moment of uncomplicated progress, scholars from a variety of fields have argued that it was not motivated by the court's desire to redress racial suffering. Rather, the court ended legal segregation to improve the country's international image at the start of the Cold War. To borrow from legal scholar Derrick Bell, *Brown v. Board of Education* was a moment of "interest convergence," a moment in which the pursuit of racial justice received a favorable decision because it coincided with the interests of whites.

Today, we no longer live under legal segregation. This fact has led many to argue that we have found our way to a post-racial nation. And yet, racial disparity abounds.

In this millennium, people of color are disproportionately imprisoned. People of color are less likely than whites to receive needed health services. Wealth disparity also exceeds the normal markers of success. "The Ever-Growing Gap: Failing To Address the Status Quo Will Drive the Racial Wealth Divide for Centuries to Come," published in 2016 by the Corporation for Economic Development and the Institute for Policy Studies, states that the average black family would need 228 years to build the wealth of the average white family.

One of the more popular—but fallacious—explanations for these disparities is the myth of black pathology. As with medical pathology, from which the concept derives, black pathology describes a condition in which a deviation from healthy behavior causes problems. In the case of black pathology, aspects of black culture, for example, the behaviors and values of black people, are believed to be the cause of racial disparity. According to some proponents, oppressive conditions shaped black culture, but black culture has remained stalled even though time has healed legal and social oppression. Other proponents claim the recognition of historically oppressive conditions has no bearing on the contemporary moment. Regardless of history, poor black communities are deemed the source or reason for ill conditions.

Putting aside the ways this myth reduces black people to a monolith, we should note that white participation within black cultural production or the adoption of values and behaviors associated with the black community is seldom enough to precipitate consequence. Whether we look at the phenomenon of Elvis or the contemporary embrace of rap music, white audiences continue to enjoy black culture with few, if any, of the consequences that proponents of black pathology associate with it. More tellingly, illicit behavior, no matter how vile, has proven to be an insufficient guarantor of long-term consequence for white people.

The same cannot be said for people of color. Drug usage, for instance, cuts across race and class, and, yet, poor communities of color are disproportionately policed and convicted for these offenses. These convictions often lead to imprisonment, which, in turn, leads to social and economic disenfranchisement upon release. What initially is seen to be the consequence of culture— or, to quote Paul Ryan, the "tailspin of culture"—is nothing less than a systemic imbalance in how communities are policed, protected, and judged.

Put more simply, to be a person of color in the United States increases the chance of a small mistake rising to catastrophe. Even worse, this threat does not require black men and women to make a mistake; consequences are suffered even when no crime has been committed. And despite its inconsistent applications across racial lines, the myth of cultural pathology has become the excuse upon which disparity is explicated and the American project exonerated.

The installation of pathology is not unique to this moment. In fact, the ease with which we accept pathology as truth is predicated upon the frequency of its installation across the past 200 years. If racist terms such as jezebel, buck, zip coon, and sambo have been removed from the American lexicon, the particular grammars[6] or ways that both the state and white communities come to know people of color have not. Nor are their installations unique to those who seek to diminish African Americans. To the contrary, pathological assignment can be found within the work

---

6   Hortense J. Spillers, "Mama's baby, papa's maybe: An American grammar book." *Diacritics* 17, no. 2 (1987): 64–81.

of historians and social scientists endeavoring to prove stereotypes of African Americans to be a both fallacious and corrosive force throughout this nation's history.

In his 1959 *Slavery: A Problem in American Institutional and Intellectual Life,* Stanley Elkins argued that the psychological impact of slavery on black men reduced them to childlike sambos and, in doing so, evacuated a great deal of misinformation spread by slavery apologists and Dunning School historians.[7] Yet, for all its intended good, the argument retains—indeed, maintains—the insidious idea that slavery created the conditions through which black pathology emerged.

Enslaved men were not the endlessly resilient survivors of slavery's violent and vile conditions. They were, instead, a series of conjoined adjectives: "Docile but irresponsible, loyal but lazy, humble but chronically given to lying and stealing." Following Elkins's description, it is not hard to imagine someone arguing that racial disparity both before and after 1865 was the consequence of uneven social development among races. Indeed, this was the case.

As early as the sixties, social scientists such as Daniel Patrick Moynihan and Kenneth Clark and journalists such as Rowland Evans and Robert Novak published reports on cultural pathologies that were believed to explain poverty across generations. By the seventies, historians had disproven Elkins's thesis, but diagnoses of pathology remained in both social science and the popular press. Much like Elkins's argument, these reports effectively shifted the location of deprivation but failed to excise pathological assignments. More simply, the black community was no longer thought to be biologically inferior; rather, it was believed to be socially and culturally stalled.

---

7   Stanley M. Elkins, *Slavery: A Problem in American Institutional and Intellectual Life* (Chicago: University of Chicago Press Books, 1987).

By the eighties and well into the nineties, concepts of the "underclass" became the primary hinge through which pathology was bolted to the black community. This was true even while many of these studies ostensibly turned to class. As David Theo Goldberg argues in *Racist Culture: Philosophy and the Politics of Meaning,* "The idea of project housing has . . . come to stand throughout 'the West' as the central mark of racially constituted urban pathology," out of which emerged a variety of newly invented stereotypes such as the welfare queen and the super predator. By contrast, poor white communities during this period were often framed as the victims of industry and a diminished economy. Whether we look at the Rust Belt, which describes a geographical area various industries once utilized and have now abandoned, or the xenophobic and unfounded notion that immigrants take jobs from U.S.-born laborers, poor white communities seldom come up against the idea that white culture is to blame for unemployment and poverty.

Whatever the historical or sociological reasoning, a single assertion continued to surface across myriad reports and across time: African Americans were the makers of their own deprivation—even as study after study proved the continued existence of institutional racism. Today, calls for African Americans to focus on "black-on-black crime," draw from this tradition, not statistics. Such calls ignore more recent work including the 2015 report from the Center for Contemporary Families responding to previous assertions of black pathology: In "Moynihan's Half Century: Have We Gone to Hell in a Hand Basket?" the authors found that a single-parent family structure, the perennial boogeyman of reactionaries, does not lead to an increase in juvenile crime or inequality. [8]

8   Jeffrey Hayes and Philip Cohen, "Moynihan's half century: Have we gone to hell in a hand basket?," *Council on Contemporary Families,* March 5, 2015.

To diminish objections to police violence, these calls also conflate separate issues—an understanding echoed by Brittney Cooper, a women's and gender studies and Africana studies professor:

> The continued focus on black-on-black crime is a diversionary tactic, whose goal is to suggest that black people don't have the right to be outraged about police violence in vulnerable black communities, because those communities have a crime problem. The Black Lives Matter movement acknowledges the crime problem, but it refuses to locate that crime problem as a problem of black pathology.[9]

Recent calls for patriotism are equally diversionary, and like calls that ask protesters to focus on crime, they miss a simple fact of history: the seizure of rights by people of color has never come from quiet acquiescence. Writing in 1845, Frederick Douglass captured the need for seizure in his eponymous narrative when he told his audience, "You have seen how a man was made a slave; you shall see how a slave was made a man."[10] Eighty years later, Elise Johnson McDougald took up the work begun by formerly enslaved women like Harriet Jacobs. In her essay "The Double Task: The Struggle of Negro Women for Sex and Race Emancipation,"[11] she refused the vile stereotypes that had long been thought to be the biological destiny of black women and urged readers to recognize the rich history of black women who had and continued to create

9   Brittney Cooper, "11 major misconceptions about the Black Lives Matter movement," *Cosmopolitan,* September 8, 2015.

10   Frederick Douglass, *Narrative of the Life of Frederick Douglass* (Boston: The Anti-Slavery Office, 1849).

11   Elise Johnson McDougald, "The double task: The struggle of negro women for sex and race emancipation," *The New Negro: An Interpretation,* ed. Alain Locke (New York: Simon & Schuster, 1999), 369–384.

lives in the midst of both racial and gender oppression. What these examples demonstrate is that black citizenship and its liberties have been made by, rather than given to, African Americans.

Today, intersectionality is the term for interrogations of this overlap between race and gender. Legal scholar and critical race theorist Kimberlé Crenshaw first introduced this term in her groundbreaking work from the late eighties that further expanded our ability to understand how race and gender form a network of oppression. Yet, the demands of people of color for racial justice often continue to be dismissed on the basis that equality can be maintained only by a colorblind approach to law and nation.

This nation, however, is not colorblind. It has never been colorblind. To paraphrase Keeanga-Yamahtta Taylor, a social activist and professor of African American Studies at Princeton University, the absence of racial insult does not evidence the absence of racial discrimination. To treat these absences as synonymous is to reveal colorblind models as little more than tactics through which the state and its citizens disavow the presence of continued racism. To singularly confront overt acts of racism, as colorblind models suggest, is to dismantle individuals' ability to confront covert racism.

This approach also enabled Ohioan and former Donald Trump campaign chair Kathy Miller to say,

> I don't think there was any racism before Obama got elected ... You've had every opportunity. It was given to you ... You've had the same schools everybody else went to. [12]

---

12   Paul Lewis and Tom Silverstone, "Ohio Trump campaign chair Kathy Miller says there was 'no racism' before Obama," *The Guardian*, September 22, 2016.

Miller's assertion illuminates how colorblind approaches obscure the operations of contemporary inequality. It also ignores how proximity and affluence have not been able to inoculate communities of color from both racial limits and animus.

Even after *Brown v. Board of Education,* people of color have not had "every opportunity." In the 60-plus years since the Supreme Court desegregated schools, educational inequality persists. In his 2001 report, "American Schooling And Educational Inequality: A Forecast for the 21st Century"[13] published in the journal *Sociology of Education,* Adam Gamoran foresaw a continuing decline in black and white educational inequality throughout the twenty-first century, but has since acknowledged that communities of color remain at a structural disadvantage. "Black Girls Matter: Pushed Out, Overpoliced and Underprotected,"[14] by Columbia Law School also found that girls of color suffer harsher punishment and are six times more likely to be suspended than their white peers, and black boys are three times more likely to be suspended than white boys.

The Georgetown Center on Education and the Workforce published its study of 4,400 postsecondary institutions "Separate & Unequal: How Higher Education Reinforces the Intergenerational Reproduction of White Racial Privilege."[15] Even though minority students have better access to higher education than ever before,

---

13 Adam Gamoran, "American schooling and educational inequality: A forecast for the 21st century," Sociology of Education, no. 74 (2001): 135-153.

14 Kimberlé Williams Crenshaw, Priscilla Ocen, and Jyoti Nanda, "Black girls matter: Pushed out, overpoliced, underprotected," Center for Intersectionality and Social Policy Studies and African American Policy Forum, 2015.

15 Anthony P. Carnevale and Jeff Strohl, "Separate & unequal: How higher education reinforces the intergenerational reproduction of white racial privilege," Center on Education and the Workforce, Georgetown University, July 31, 2013.

their research shows that African American and Latin American students are being channeled into open-access two- and four-year colleges at the undergraduate level while white students are encouraged to apply to more selective colleges. And obstacles do not end once a person of color enters college. "What Happens Before? A Field Experiment Exploring How Pay and Representation Differentially Shape Bias on the Pathway Into Organizations"[16] from the *Journal of Applied Psychology* shows that faculty are more likely to ignore inquiries about research opportunities when posed by women and people of color than when posed by white males. Equally dire findings can be found within employment.

In *Knocking the Hustle: Against the Neoliberal Turn in Black Politics,*[17] Lester K. Spence analyzes the job opportunities of the pre-Barack Obama nineties. Whereas the vast majority of white employment seekers were placed in positions that included job security, stable hours, safe working conditions, and benefits, approximately 75 percent of the jobs in which African Americans and Latin Americans were placed during this same period did not. In fact, Spence found that "three out of every five jobs that were added among black and Latino populations were bad jobs," offering "very low wages, unstable hours, little to no job security, little to no dignity, no due process, unsafe working conditions, and little to no benefits."

Thus, directly contra Kathy Miller's claims, people of color in the pre-Obama nineties did not fail to take advantage of job opportunities. Rather, the employment opportunities available to

---

16 Katherine Milkman, Modupe Akinola, and Dolly Chugh, "What happens before? A field experiment exploring how pay and representation differentially shape bias on the pathway into organizations," *Journal of Applied Psychology* 100, no. 6 (2015): 1678-1712.

17 Lester K. Spence, *Knocking the Hustle: Against the Neoliberal Turn in Black Politics* (New York: Punctum Books, 2015).

job seekers were, in part, determined by race. Furthermore, such determinations led to jobs that amplified disenfranchisement within African American and Latinx communities.

Colorblindism, however, is not the exclusive domain of reactionary dismissal; it has also bankrupted goodwill efforts such as empathy. Even though it can be and often is a powerful means through which we come to better see and understand those who live at a distance from us, empathy is dangerous when used as the means through which difference is erased. As Saidiya V. Hartman argues in *Scenes of Subjection: Terror, Slavery, and Self-Making in Nineteenth-Century America*,[18] empathy always threatens to become the method through which the powerful hijack the experiences of oppressed communities. By employing a "shared language of pain," those who are enfranchised link themselves to the kind of violence endured by institutionally marginalized communities. The danger of this is twofold: the enfranchised are allowed not only to speak for the disenfranchised, but also to center their experiences, and thereby replace marginalized experiences with their own.

When, in her 2016 Democratic National Convention speech,[19] Hillary Clinton called for Americans to "put ourselves in the shoes of" both "young black and Latino men and women who face the effects of systemic racism" and police officers, she offered listeners a shared language of pain through which to equate the violence wrought by racism with the killing of police. In doing so, she drew people of color and the police as parallel communities. They are not. Violence that manifests because of systemic racism

---

18   Saidiya V. Hartman, *Scenes of Subjection: Terror, Slavery, and Self-Making in Nineteenth-Century America* (New York: Oxford University Press, 1997).

19   Hillary Clinton, "Hillary Clinton's DNC speech: full text," *CNN*, July 29, 2016.

and the threat of violence police officers face are distinct phenomena. Both are tragic, but to link them rhetorically and temporally, as Clinton did, demonstrates a fundamental misunderstanding of what people mean when they invoke ideas such as systemic racism and white supremacy.

Whether we look at its utility for smuggling in older iterations of racism or the ways it encourages individuals to be uncritical of structural racism, colorblindism is central to the maintenance of white supremacy. At best, it mistakes good intentions for good ends—even as dire consequences disproportionately befall communities of color. At worst, it is the method through which the acknowledgement of racial difference becomes antithetical to the American project—even as such acknowledgements are necessary for rooting out today's most insidious inequalities.

These are just a few of the issues that surround Kaepernick's decision not to stand. They are the issues we ignore when we recommend that high school athletes not do the same. To sit or to take a knee is to move against tactics that seek to blind us to racial disenfranchisement and violence. Such acts are neither simple abstentions nor simply disrespectful.

Rather, these acts of radical insertion seek to halt narratives that erase black lives politically, socially, and physically. And in doing so, they help many of us to recognize that, even though the vagueness of this country's foundational creed opens up an ideological space through which people of color have inserted themselves, our nation's founding documents—the colonial, state, and national laws that both establish and sustain our lives—have been much clearer about whose rights and desires should be protected. Indeed, Kaepernick's opponents would do well to consult *American Slavery, American Freedom*,[20] wherein Perry Miller's student Edmund S. Morgan famously argued that American slavery was the predicate upon which (white) American freedom was won.

Michael Sasha King is a scholar of African American literature and music who specializes in the period between 1865 and the present.

---

20   Edmund S. Morgan, *American Slavery, American Freedom* (New York: W. W. Norton & Co., 1975).

Deva Woodly

#BlackLivesMatter and the Democratic Necessity of Social Movements

What Active Citizenship Can Look Like
and What it Can Accomplish

> I hold that a little rebellion now and then is a good thing, and
> as necessary in the political world as storms in the physical.
> —*Thomas Jefferson, Letter to James Madison (1787)*

> We who believe in freedom cannot rest.—*Ella Baker (1964)*[1]

Social movements are often regarded as potentially hazardous
disruptions, uprisings that interfere with the normal mechanisms
of politics—insurgencies that must be either repressed or swiftly
reincorporated into the regular legislative process. In 2016,
three years after its emergence, President Barack Obama chided
the Movement for Black Lives by saying that it had been "really
effective at bringing attention to problems" but claiming, "once
you've highlighted an issue and brought it to people's attention .
. . [and] elected officials or people who are in a position to start
bringing about change are ready to sit down with you, then you
can't just keep on yelling at them."[2] He went on to say, "the value

---

1   Fundi: The Story of Ella Baker, dir. by Joanne Grant (Turner Classic Movies, 1981).

2   Michael D. Shear and Liam Stack, "Obama says movements like Black Lives Matter
'can't just keep on yelling,'" *The New York Times,* April 23, 2016.

of social movements and activism is to get you at the table, to get you in the room, and then to figure out: how is the problem to be solved."

Obama's view is a common one, but it is also incorrect. The value of movements is something much more profound. Movements are what keep democracy from falling irrevocably into the pitfalls of bureaucracy and oligarchy described by Max Weber, chiefly: dehumanization, expropriation, and stagnation. This is important because democracy is more than the institutional—largely electoral—framework that is commonly associated with it. In truth, democracy demands a broad political orientation toward participation and citizenship from "the people" who are to govern. A democracy where people have come to believe that voting is the only kind of participation that matters; that their vote, in any case, doesn't count; that the system is fundamentally "rigged"; that those who govern are not "like them," and worse, are unresponsive, is a polity that will struggle (and perhaps fail) to bear the burden and responsibility of self-governance. If citizens, from whose authorization the legitimacy of democratic government arises, come to believe that their capacity to act as authors of their collective fate is a fiction, then what follows is what I call a politics of despair.

I argue that the force that counteracts the Weberian pitfalls of bureaucratization and oligarchy and which can counteract the politics of despair by "repoliticiz[ing] public life,"[3] is social movements. Social movements infuse the essential elements of pragmatic imagination, social intelligence, and democratic experimentation into public spheres that are ailing, and have become nonresponsive, stagnant, and/or closed. They are necessary, not

---

3   Iris Marion Young, *Justice and the Politics of Difference* (Princeton: Princeton University Press, 2011).

only to address the concerns of those engaging in public protest, nor only for the ethical purpose of achieving more just conditions for all, but also, for the health and survival of democracy, as such. The Movement for Black Lives is a contemporary movement that shows us the dimensions of the essential function that social movements play in democracy.

THE POLITICAL CONTEXT

The graphic and bewildering 2016 electoral contest, and its surprising outcome, seemed to make the world anew overnight, especially for the 73 million voters who had cast their ballots for someone other than Trump. Those Americans woke on November 9, 2016 to what suddenly seemed a new and uncertain era. However, the political tumult that gave rise to the contentious and surprising election cycle began much earlier. Already, the twenty-first century had begun to put the lie to the notion in the nineties that America and the world had reached "the end of history," in which the liberal international order and increasing development would lead to ever growing tolerance and prosperity. Instead, the first year of the new millennium showed us the birth of a new form of international conflict and the first decade ushered in the largest financial collapse the world had seen since the thirties. During what was dubbed the Great Recession, one quarter of American families lost at least 75 percent of their wealth, and more than half lost at least 25 percent.[4] As with almost every indicator of American well-being, for African Americans, the news was even worse: the median net worth of black families fell 53 percent (National Association of Real Estate Brokers, 2013). The national unemploy-

---

4   Fabian T. Pfeffer, Sheldon Danziger, and Robert F. Schoeni, "Wealth disparities before and after the Great Recession," National Poverty Center Working Paper Series, April 2013.

ment rate had climbed to above 10 percent, but for blacks, the rate topped 17 percent.[5] When the wave of job loss began to recede in 2013, it left in its wake occupations that did not provide as much stability or income as the ones that had been swept away.

But the economic devastation of the Great Recession and the precarity that it laid bare was not the only tumult testing the temerity of American Dreamers by 2016. Already, a black teenager named Trayvon Martin had been hunted and gunned down by a vigilante as he walked home in a small town in Florida. Already, Rekia Boyd had been shot dead by an off-duty cop on a burger run, while standing in her neighborhood park. Eric Garner, a black man selling loose cigarettes on a New York City street corner, and pleading "I can't breathe," had already been choked to death on video by a police patrolman. Twelve-year-old Tamir Rice, mistaken for a twenty-year-old man, had been slaughtered by law enforcement while playing behind a community center. Already, Sandra Bland had been disappeared into the cell where she would die for behaving as though she were free during a traffic stop. And, Mike Brown's cooling body had already lain uncovered on the hot concrete for four hours after being shot dead by a police officer who claimed the unarmed teen looked like a "demon." In each case, the killings were deemed justified. The perpetrators left free.

The justice system's shrug of acceptance in the face of the violent, unnecessary deaths of black people at the hands of vigilantes and the state mirrored the unconcern that seemed to suffuse all the institutions of power as they witnessed the post-recession suffering of ordinary people of all colors, seeming to do lit-

---

5   Carolyn B. Maloney and Charles E. Schumer, "Weekly economic digest," report from the U.S. Congress Joint Economic Committee, March 17, 2010.

tle or nothing in response. Indeed, in the second decade of the twenty-first century, the world had already witnessed a series of uprisings demanding democratic accountability and economic fairness around the world. This context made organizer Alicia Garza's hastily typed cry that "black lives should matter" one that entered the political environment resonant with grief and gravitas. Garza's fellow organizer, Patrisse Cullors, put the exhortation behind a hashtag that yet another organizer and collaborator, Opal Tometi, pushed onto what were in 2012, the lesser used social media platforms of Twitter and Tumblr. #BlackLivesMatter quickly diffused across social media and became a part of national discourse, and later, a rallying cry for mass mobilizations in the streets. But what characteristics created a "political opportunity" for the political commotion that has characterized America's early twenty-first century?

THE POLITICS OF DESPAIR

Scholarly interest in the role that emotions play in social movements was piqued after the intensely emotional political work of attempting to get recognition of and redress for the AIDS crisis in the late eighties and early nineties. Veterans of that work, most notably sociologist Deborah Gould, began insisting that studying movement organizations without taking note of the emotions that motivated, animated, and complicated them, was overlooking a major part of the story of emergence, maintenance, and demobilization of movements. In 2012, Gould introduced the concept of "political despair," which she described as a "feeling of inefficacy and hopelessness, the sense that nothing will ever change, no matter what some imagined collective 'we' does to try to bring change."[6] Gould goes on to describe political despair as a part of the "affective landscape of the early twenty-first century." But political despair is more than a public mood,[7] it is also a politics, that is, "the activity through which relatively large and permanent groups of people determine what they will collectively do, settle how they will live together, and decide their future." Politics "concerns all aspects of institutional organization, public action, social practices and habits, and cultural meanings insofar as they are potentially subject to collective evaluation and decision-making."[8] For citizens, a politics of despair is characterized by a lack of institutional investment and public trust, suspicion of the social practices and habits of others in the polity, cultural meanings that are illegible across difference, as well as deep cynicism about the possibility of political efficacy. For governors, a politics of despair is characterized by a Weberian retreat to bureaucratized oligarchy particularly marked by either indifference or inability to respond to the concerns of constituents.

Evidence that the United States can be described as in the grips of a politics of despair can be found in several trends that have been intensifying for decades; namely, (a) rising inequality, (b) declining political trust, (c) declining interpersonal trust, (d) declining civic knowledge, (e) declining and stratified political participation, and (f) declining political efficacy. The data demonstrating each of these trends is voluminous and robust. Social and economic inequality has been rising since the mid-twentieth cen-

---

6   Deborah B. Gould, "Political despair," *Politics and the Emotions: The Affective Turn in Contemporary Political Studies*, eds. Paul Hoggett and Simon Thompson (New York: Continuum International Publishing Group, 2012), 95–114.

7   Hanna Fenichel Pitkin, "Justice: On relating private and public," *Political Theory* 9, no. 3 (1981): 327–52.

8   *Young, Justice* (2011).

tury, with income inequality currently more stark than it has been since the Gilded Age imploded in 1928. The top one percent of income earners have seen their share of total income rise from 8.9 percent in 1973 to 21.2 percent in 2014.[9] This startling proportion doesn't capture the fact that income growth during that time has accrued almost exclusively to the top one percent of income earners.[10] The data on the increasing wealth gap is even more severe, with America's upper-income families possessing 70 times the wealth of lower-income families and seven times the wealth of middle-income families, the largest gap recorded by the Federal Reserve in the 30 years it has been collecting data.[11] When these numbers are parsed by race and ethnicity, the already wide divide reveals itself to be cavernous, with the median wealth of white households increasing by 2.4 percent, from $138,600 to $141,900, between 2010 and 2013, while Hispanics' median wealth decreased by 14.3 percent, from $16,000 to $13,700, and black households' fell 33.7 percent, from $16,600 to $11,000. These gaps in income and wealth are not unique among indicators of well-being.[12] Egregious and persistent gaps in class,[13] race,[14] and gender are evident in everything from education, to physical safety, health, and contact with disciplining institutions.

9   Drew Desilver, "The many ways to measure economic inequality," Pew Research Center, September 22, 2015.

10   Emmanuel Saez, "U.S. top one percent of income earners hit new high in 2015 amid strong economic growth," Washington Center for Equitable Growth, July 1, 2016.

11   Richard Fry and Rakesh Kochhar, "America's wealth gap between middle-income and upper-income families is widest on record," Pew Research Center, December 17, 2014.

12   Anthony B. Atkinson, *Inequality: What Can Be Done?* (Cambridge, MA: Harvard University Press, 2015).

13   Thomas Piketty, *The Economics of Inequality* (Cambridge, MA: Harvard University Press, 2015).

14   Eduardo Bonilla-Silva, *Racism Without Racists: Colorblind Racism and the Persistence of Racial Inequality in America* (New York: Rowman & Littlefield Publishers, 2013).

Additionally, trust in government is at an historic low. According to the Pew Research Center, only 19 percent of respondents trust the government in Washington to do what is right "just about always" or "most of the time."[15] By comparison, 73 percent of Americans answered this question affirmatively in 1958; 49 percent did so in 2001. Questions about individual institutions reveal similar skepticism. The only institutions that a majority of Americans trust are the military (73 percent) and police (56 percent).[16] Only 36 percent trust the president and the Supreme Court, 23 percent trust the criminal justice system and organized labor, 20 percent trust newspapers, and 9 percent trust Congress.

Alongside this lack of trust in institutions, Americans have become much more likely to sort themselves by party sympathies now than two decades ago.[17] This partisan sorting is not limited to issue positions, with more Democrats and Republicans espousing policy preferences that align with their chosen party, but also includes social sorting. Democrats and Republicans are now less likely to participate in the same entertainment, live in the same neighborhoods, or consume the same goods.[18] Perhaps because of this sorting, there has also been a stunning increase in personal antipathy between Democrats and Republicans, with 86 percent of Democrats reporting that they have an "unfavorable" view of Republicans and 55 percent "very unfavorable." Likewise, 91 percent of Republicans report that they view Democrats unfavorably

15   "Beyond distrust: How Americans view their government," Pew Research Center, November 23, 2015.

16   Jim Norman, "Americans' confidence in institutions stays low," *Gallup News,* June 13, 2016.

17   Arthur Lupia, *Uninformed: Why People Seem to Know So Little About Politics and What We Can Do About It* (New York: Oxford University Press, 2015).

18   Michael Dimock, Jocelyn Kiley, Scott Keeter, and Carroll Doherty, "Political polarization and personal life," *Political Polarization and the American Public,* Pew Research Center, June 12, 2014, 42–55.

and 58 percent very unfavorably.[19] The personal antipathy between partisans hints at an even more troubling phenomenon: Americans' declining trust in each other generally. In 1974, 46 percent of Americans reported that they trusted most people; by 2012, only 33 percent said the same, with millennials reporting less trust in others than any other generation.[20] To make matters worse, Americans know less about how their government is structured and how it is supposed to function than ever before, with only one-quarter of Americans able to name the three branches of government and one-third of Americans unable to name any of them.[21]

These changes in fortunes, trust, and knowledge have taken a toll on the belief that democratic government can be responsive to most citizens, producing dramatic and widespread disillusionment with the idea that political participation by ordinary citizens can create positive change. This bleak view of the effects of traditional political participation is not merely the result of a cynical outlook. Americans have good reason to doubt their ability to affect national politics. Political scientists have shown that government responsiveness is stratified by socioeconomic status.[22] Is it any wonder, then, that political participation is stratified in the same way, with the wealthy and educated much more likely to contribute their "money, skills, and time" in the political arena than those who

---

19 "Partisanship and political animosity in 2016," Pew Research Center, June 22, 2016.

20 Jean M. Twenge, W. Keith Campbell and Nathan T. Carter, "Declines in trust in others and confidence in institutions among American adults and late adolescents," *Psychological Science* 25, no. 10 (2014): 1–12.

21 Lupia, *Uninformed* (2015).

22 Martin Gilens and Benjamin I. Page, "Testing theories of American politics: Elites, interest groups, and average citizens," *Perspectives on Politics* 12, no. 3 (2014): 564–581; Marc J. Hetherington and Thomas J. Rudolph, *Why Washington Won't Work: Polarization, Political Trust, and the Governing Crisis* (Chicago: University of Chicago Press, 2015).

have fewer resources, but need more responsiveness?[23] For black Americans, the reality of stratified representation is even more severe. Though the civil rights movements of the fifties and sixties opened pathways for more African Americans to participate in the political process and elect some members of the group as political representatives, "the price of the ticket" has been electoral capture by one increasingly unresponsive party, and the decline of a politics dedicated to confronting racial inequality head on.[24] Given these realities, the breadth of the crisis we now face is profound.

A series of pointed and urgent questions arise from these facts: what helps members of the polity to recover from the cynicism wrought by insufficiently responsive governance? What reminds us of the power of the public sphere? What causes governing officials to be responsive to new or neglected constituencies and attentive to their causes? What helps us to feel that our opinions and political actions matter—that "we the people" have power? What makes a citizenry both believe and act on behalf of the belief that "another world is possible?"

The answer is social movements. And the Movement for Black Lives is a powerful case that shows what organized members of the polity can do. The politics of despair need not persist. Indeed, if democracy is to survive as a form of governance, it cannot persist. Social movements can repoliticize public life because they remind people both of what active citizenship can look like and what it can accomplish. As such, social movements repoliticize public life

---

23   Kay Lehman Schlozman, Sidney Verba and Henry E. Brady, *The Unheavenly Chorus: Unequal Political Voice and the Broken Promise of American Democracy* (Princeton: Princeton University Press, 2012).

24   Paul Frymer, Uneasy Alliances: Race and Party Competition in America (Princeton: Princeton University Press, 2010); Fredrick Harris, *The Price of the Ticket: Barack Obama and the Rise and Decline of Black Politics* (New York: Oxford University Press, 2014).

by serving the following critical democratic functions. First, they stimulate pragmatic imagination. That is, because social movements seek to raise questions and seek remedies for ills that have gone overlooked, they cause us to look at the world with new eyes and imagine how it can and should be improved. Second, social movements remind us of the necessity for democratic experimentation. Democratic experimentation is a concept that I take from John Dewey.[25] It refers to the "reconstruction" and "reorganization" of experience based on the conviction that we should avoid repeating past mistakes by seeking to advance our understanding of and experience in the world by changing our approach to acknowledged problems. Third, social movements model a politically useful democratic intelligence. "The office of intelligence in every problem," Dewey writes, "is to effect a working connection between old habits, customs, institutions, beliefs, and new conditions."[26] This is what social movements do. They take up the responsibility to "make democracy a living reality" by first, bringing new issues (or ways of looking at issues) to light. Second, interrupting our old habits, while making connections between problems and possible solutions. And third, by organizing, which means causing people to demonstrably commit themselves to political action. Finally, social movements teach participants political efficacy while also modeling it for the general polity.

Deva Woodly is an assistant professor of politics at the New School for Social Research and editor of Race/isms on Public Seminar.

---

25 John Dewey, *Democracy and Education* (New York: The Free Press, 1997).

26 John Dewey, *Liberalism and Social Action* (New York: Prometheus Books, 2000).

Mitchell Kosters

Escaping the Logic(s) of White Supremacy

The Practice of Oppositional Thought

In her article "Indigeneity, Settler Colonialism, White Supremacy," Andrea Smith advances the argument that there is no monolithic white supremacy. Rather, white supremacy should best be understood as a phenomenon "constituted by separate and distinct, but still interrelated, logics."[1] She identifies three different racial schematics corresponding to the different strands of white supremacist ideology. These are "slaveability/anti-black racism, which anchors capitalism ... [the] genocide [of indigenous peoples], which anchors colonialism ... [and] orientalism, which anchors war."[2] The most significant part of this formulation is its breadth; white supremacy is not unitary, but composed of multiple fluid networks of relationships. It operates based on the contingent needs of the specific (white) power structure. There is no need to expect that—in such a globally expansive network as capitalist-colonial white supremacy—all racially marginalized people will be exploited in identical, or even generally homogenous, ways. Indeed, as racial-colonial relationships become more entrenched, differently oppressed sets of marginal subjects become integrated into the white supremacist system such that their personal success depends on the continued marginalization of others.

---

1 Andrea Smith, "Indigeneity, settler colonialism, white supremacy," *Racial Formation in the Twenty-First Century,* ed. Daniel Martinez HoSang (Berkeley: University of California Press, 2012), 67.

2 Ibid., 68.

Although unmentioned in Smith's work, an example of this sort of situation is the relationship between French colonial power and its Senegalese subjects in colonial West Africa. Under the *Évolués* (literally "evolved") system, French authorities allowed some native Senegalese access to education, status, and the right to vote in return for loyalty to French administration. These newly legitimized French citizens in turn went on to operate much of the empire's African bureaucracy and played a key role in French domination of West Africa. More than mere capitulation, though, Smith believes that this multiplicitous white supremacy presents an incredible danger for the general capacities of an organized counter-power. In her own words, "Our survival strategies and resistance to white supremacy are set by the system of white supremacy itself."[3] In other words, the ways in which different people have historically responded to the threat of white racial domination have actually themselves participated in the upholding of white supremacist power.

This formulation, I think, is largely accurate. It still leaves us, however, with the age old question of political organization: what is to be done? Smith's essay generally shies from advice on practical organizing, directing itself, rather, towards a scholarly critique of ethnic and indigenous studies. By turning to academic Mia White, however, I believe that we can rectify this deficit, flipping the logic of white supremacy on its head. Central to White's thought is a matrix of three concepts, which she believes organize and govern all social interaction: institutions, histories, and spaces. "Institutions" are the structures and mechanisms that govern the lives of individuals and work to enforce social order. White emphasizes race as a pow-

---

3   Ibid.,70.

erful example of this kind of construct. "History" is the end result of our contested, dialogical processes of meaning making. Finally, "spaces" are the actual material and epistemological grounds upon which institutions and histories exert themselves. Spaces are those places where living subjects coexist with one another. As social and affective phenomena, White's spaces have a rhythm of their own. They produce many series of physical and emotional links between subjects engaging in the same given place. These ties are incredibly powerful and have the capacity to dramatically alter the ways that people interact with each other and with the larger spatial imaginary. No space is fully ensconced within the logics of institutions and histories. Rather, the very nature of all spaces assures that they are basically creative and productive planes. Most important here is that marginal subjects—those oppressed by racial institutions and exclusionary histories—can and do co-opt spaces that are largely designed for their exploitation.

The multiple white supremacies of Smith's essay do not seem nearly as all encompassing when seen through White's viewpoint. By sorting all racialized subjects into the same imperial space, colonial administrators are in fact hastening the creation of bonded, affective relationships between those under their thumb, thereby hastening the creation of a consciousness among "the exploited," regardless of the specific form their oppression takes.

This is not to say that the mere fact of "being together" is enough to destroy white supremacist power. This amounts to magical thinking. Spatial and epistemological proximity only create the capacity for resistance, not the energy for it, much less any opening in the edifice of colonial-imperial institutions and histories. The type of affective thinking proposed by White is a first step to a larger project of solidarity, however. White supremacy relies on strict hierarchies of perceived ability and capacity. Through our interaction with each other in racist or colonial spaces, the strict demarcations imposed by white supremacy begin to blur a little. Affect can take over (at least a little) from ideology and we can begin to create new forms of knowledge and new ways of knowing and seeing the world.

Elizabeth Povinelli makes the distinction between the knowledge of ideas and the knowledge of affects much clearer. For Povinelli, "An idea represents something while an affect does not. An affect is not nothing, but it is also not something in the same way as an extrinsic or intrinsic idea. An affect is a force of existing (*vis existendi*) that is neither the realized thing (an idea) nor the accomplishment of the thing (*potentia agendi*)."[4] Affect represents "the perpetual variation between *vis existendi* and *potentia agendi*—between striving to persevere and any actual idea or action that emerges from this striving—provides a space of potentiality where new forms of life can emerge."[5] This is a knowledge different from the "rational," "logical," racial-functionalist approach taken by white supremacists. It is an emotional, vulnerable knowledge that is open to dissent, subversion, and alterity, the kind of knowledge that comes from an internalization of "the Other" and "the Outside." This knowledge treats all human subjects as co-creators of communal space, rather than subordinate objects to be acted upon. Affective knowledge is a *democratic* knowledge, while the ideational, ideological knowledge of white supremacy seeks only order according to its presupposed first principles.

---

4   Elizabeth A. Povinelli, *Economies of Abandonment: Social Belonging and Endurance in Late Liberalism* (Durham, NC: Duke University Press, 2011), 9.

5   Ibid.

This sort of counter-knowledge, and more importantly the actual practice of oppositional thought, is especially important as white supremacy strengthens its power, most recently signaled by the election of Donald Trump in the United States and the general surge in support for the far right in Europe. As refugees from Africa, the Middle East, and beyond pour into these areas, the spaces they inhabit will become increasingly politically charged. With all these racially marginalized subjects inhabiting approximately the same places, it will become increasingly easier to see through the multitudinous network apparatus of Smith's white supremacy, so long as we are adequately prepared for the challenge. The partisans of white supremacist power certainly are, weaponizing history and institutions to keep their authority unchecked. In order to mount a proper response to this challenge, those committed to anti-racism need to begin to change their thinking. While solidarity has played a large role in the self-expression of the activist left, this has largely been a symbolic gesture. True solidarity means changing the ways we understand ourselves. It means becoming affective, rather than rational, subjects—becoming truly comfortable with vulnerability and change. More than this, thinking spatially as White does, we need to imbricate our very subjectivities with those foreign to us, producing new spaces wherein the institutions and histories of racial domination have less grasp. In doing this, we challenge not only colonial and imperial violence, but the entire Enlightenment subjectivity of Western superiority. The spaces composing the institutions of genocide, orientalism, and anti-black racism are not fully fixed. The guards are not always watching. The walls can be torn down.

Mitchell Kosters is an M.A. history student at the New School for Social Research.

Mindy Thompson Fullilove et al.

Before Charlottesville There Was Jamestown

We don't know the exact day the British man-of-war, *The White Lion,* arrived in August of 1619, bringing Africans to be sold into bondage. We do know that its arrival roped the British North American colonies into the institution of slavery and the heinous trade that supplied it. We also know that, realizing there were profits to made from slavery, slave owners and slave traders set about justifying this crime against humanity by saying that Africans were not fully human.

The "not fully human people" recognized the insanity of this proposition. A "Petition of a Great Number of Negroes" to the Massachusetts House of Representatives, in 1777, stated:

> The Petition of a great number of Negroes who are detained in a state of Slavery in the Bowels of a free and Christian County Humbly Shewing: That your petitioners apprehend that they have in common with all other Men, a natural and unalienable right to that freedom, which the great Parent of the Universe hath bestowed equally on all Mankind, and which they have never forfeited by any compact or agreement whatever ... [1]

Despite the protests of the enslaved, the vicious lie shaped the colonies as they became states in a slave nation. The Constitution included the grim clause that those slaves were to be counted as

---

1   Howard Zinn and Anthony Arnove, *Voices of a People's History: Tenth Anniversary Edition* (New York: Seven Stories Press, 2014), 57.

"3/5s of a person." The Big Lie had other uses, the slave masters discovered. By making slight distinctions between white indentured servants and black slaves, they could set them against one another, defeating class warfare with the infamous "divide and conquer" tactic.

And that was not all: the Big Lie justified oppressing indigenous people, homosexuals, women, Jews, immigrants, and the disabled, indeed, an endless parade of those labeled "not full people." The physician in our team—Mindy Thompson Fullilove—has likened this process to the doctor's "off-label" use of medicines. In U.S. law, once a medicine is approved for a specific indication, it is legal for doctors to use it for other problems for which it seems to be effective. These are called "off-label indications." One example, from the *Pharmacy Times* (January 5, 2016), is Prazosin (Minipress), approved for treating hypertension, but also used for nightmares associated with post-traumatic stress disorder, in addition to being used as treatment for Raynaud's Disease and for poisoning due to scorpion venom. Once blacks were legally codified as 3/5s of a person, the Big Lie could be used "off-label" to stigmatize anybody.

Thus, the history of the United States includes the struggle against abolition, the struggle for women's equality, and the struggle for protections for working people, and in this process we have gone jittering back and forth between success and setback. Every success follows the creation of solid, intergroup alliances, and every setback is due, at least in part, to the potent weapon of the Big Lie.

We see this pattern in the "Unite the Right" rally held in Charlottesville, August 11 and 12, 2017, an effort by the right to push back progress on removing the Charlottesville symbols of white supremacy, which were installed in 1924, at the height of the Jim Crow era. Not only had Robert E. Lee Park been renamed Emancipation Park, but a statue of Lee was to be removed. Many organizations of the right came together, bearing symbols of the Confederacy, the Ku Klux Klan, and the Nazis, and demonstrating their contempt for blacks, Jews, immigrants, and others they saw as less than human. Whipped into a rage by the inflammatory remarks of their leaders, they clashed with counter-protesters decrying white supremacy. Tragedy followed.

The clash in Charlottesville is a predictable outcome of what happened at Jamestown. We cannot divorce ourselves from the long history of the Big Lie, but, like the last fairy at Sleeping Beauty's christening, we have the power to modify the curse. We are presented with the opportunity to use 2019, the 400th anniversary of *The White Lion*'s landing, to make our past a compass guiding us to a democratic future.

USES OF ANNIVERSARIES

Anniversaries are peculiar times, with enormous import for individuals and the groups of which they are a part. We don't have to consciously remember an anniversary for it to have power: we will stub our toe or burst out crying, our bodies doing the work of reminding us that a certain moment in the calendar has come around again. With each anniversary, we may re-engage with the past, understand it from new viewpoints, learn lessons that might have escaped us previously, and feel emotions that have just bubbled to the surface. When we can move through such a time consciously, and with others, we can draw even more benefit from the moment.

Such was the case in Nantes, one of the most prominent of the French cities, which engaged in the slave trade. It had long been recognized by the city's leaders as the major contributor to the status of the city as one of the largest, and richest, in France. But on the occasion of an important tricentennial celebration of *le code noir*—the code that established and served to regulate the slave trade and the treatment of those who were placed in bondage—major questions were posed about its problematic past. Will the place of the city as one of the international leaders of *la traite*—the traffic in slaves—be formally acknowledged as part of its otherwise glorious history?

The creation of a non-governmental organization, Le Triangle Ebene (the Ebony Triangle), provided the impetus for an international colloquium that was organized by the University of Nantes. It engaged historians, academics, and the general public in extensive discussions of the city's role in the slave trade. As is noted in one of the records of this momentous colloquium:

> *C'était la première fois en France qu'une manifestation d'une telle ampleur avait lieu sur les sujets de la traite négrière et de l'esclavage.*

> This was the first time in France that an exposition (demonstration) of this size had taken place to focus attention on the slave trade and on slavery.[2]

Pierre Perron, the artist who created the poster for the occasion, has often described it as one of the most important of his more than 50-year career. The poster enflamed the conversation,

---

2 *Anneaux de la Memoire*, retrieved from http://fracademic.com/dic.nsf/frwiki/1822497.

inciting discussions that led to creation of another association, *Les Anneaux de la Memoire*, and to the eventual creation of the Memorial to the Abolition of the Slave Trade in Nantes. That memorial is one of the most important and significant testimonies to the part a major urban area played in a horrific past, as well as to the city's evolving commitment to serve as a monument to France's devise: Liberté, Fraternité, Egalité.

We, the authors of this chapter, had the opportunity to visit the memorial in March 2018 as guests of the city of Nantes. Designed by Julian Bonder and Krzysztof Wodiczko, the memorial has two major components. The first is a plaza dotted with the names of the *negriers* (slave ships) that sailed from Nantes in more than 1,800 expeditions that transported 550,000 people from their homelands. The second part is an underground space in which slanted glass panels create the feeling of the ribs of a ship, while sharing the words of people who fought against slavery and the slave trade. The descent to the entrance of this part moves us into a darkened, narrow space, and greets us with Article 4 of the Universal Declaration of Human Rights, which declares that no one shall be held a slave. The tension is maintained as one walks through the long space, enlivened by anti-slavery words. Typical of the words on the panels is the song, "Oh Freedom," rendered in French as, "O Liberté sur moi."[3] The fundamental gift of the memorial is the physical apposition of the oppressive, long space, with the force of words that shout our longing for freedom. We are taught that we have and can continue to push against oppression, to create liberty.

DEMOCRACY FOR SURVIVAL

3   Julian Bonder, "On memory, trauma, public space, monuments, and memorials," *Places* 21, no. 1 (2009).

The story of Nantes helps us to see the role that the observance of an anniversary can play in setting a city on a path towards inclusion and democracy. Given the importance of inequality to our national discourse at this time, it behooves us to observe the momentous occasion of 1619 with the solemnity and attention it deserves. We can prepare for the anniversary by studying our history, by visiting sites that hold the stories of the past, and by talking to our elders. We can also prepare by asking museums and libraries, theater directors and orchestras to plan events and exhibitions that will give us insights we currently lack. We have time, and therefore we can make a space for this anniversary.

Nearly 400 years of division have created an apartheid society: we need a new social infrastructure to carry us through the challenges of climate change, decaying physical infrastructure, rapidly evolving jobs, underperforming schools, uneven access to health care, and lack of affordable housing. Our central task is to engage as many individuals and as many institutions in the U.S. as can be mustered to join together and move from inequality to equality, from some people being counted as 3/5s to all being counted as 5/5s. Starting now, we can prepare for the anniversary by deepening our understanding of our history, and then building new coalitions that cross divides to define and address our common needs. This will transform the curse of this Jamestown and is the work of this anniversary.

Mindy Fullilove, William Morrish, and Robert Sember are professors at The New School. Robert Fullilove is a professor at Columbia University.

Julia Ott

Slaves

The Capital That Made Capitalism

Racialized chattel slaves were the capital that made capitalism. While most theories of capitalism set slavery apart as something utterly distinct, because under slavery workers do not labor for a wage, new historical research reveals that for centuries a single economic system encompassed both the plantation and the factory.[1]

At the dawn of the industrial age commentators like Rev. Thomas Malthus could not envision that capital—an asset that is used but not consumed in the production of goods and services—could compound and diversify its forms, increasing productivity and engendering economic growth. Yet, ironically, when Malthus penned his *Essay on the Principle of Population* in 1798, the economies of Western Europe already had crawled their way out of the so-called "Malthusian trap."[2] The New World yielded vast quantities of "drug foods" like tobacco, tea, coffee, chocolate, and sugar for world markets. Europeans worked a little bit harder to satiate their hunger for these "drug foods." The luxury commodities of the seventeenth century became integrated into the new middle-class rituals like tea-drinking in the eighteenth century. By the nineteenth century, these commodities became a caloric and stimulative necessity for the denizens of the dark satanic mills. The New World yielded food for proletarians and fiber for factories

1 Sven Beckert and Seth Rockman, "How slavery led to modern capitalism: Echoes," *Bloomberg View,* January 24, 2012.

2 Thomas Malthus, *An Essay on the Principle of Population and Other Writings,* ed. by Robert Mayhew (London: Penguin Books, 2015).

at reasonable (even falling) prices. The "industrious revolution" that began in the sixteenth century set the stage for the Industrial Revolution of the late eighteenth and nineteenth centuries.[3]

But the "demand side" tells only part of the story. A new form of capital, racialized chattel slaves, proved essential for the industrious revolution—and for the industrial one that followed.

The systematic application of African slaves in staple export crop production began in the sixteenth century, with sugar in Brazil.[4] The African slave trade populated the plantations of the Caribbean, landing on the shores of the Chesapeake at the end of the seventeenth century. African slaves held the legal status of chattel: moveable, alienable property. When owners hold living creatures as chattel, they gain additional property rights: the ownership of the offspring of any chattel, and the ownership of their offspring, and so on and so forth. Chattel becomes self-augmenting capital.

While slavery had existed in human societies since prehistoric times, chattel status had never been applied so thoroughly to human beings as it would be to Africans and African Americans beginning in the sixteenth century. But this was not done easily, especially in New World regions like Britain's mainland colonies in North America where African slaves survived, worked alongside European indentured servants and landless "free" men and women, and bore offspring.

In the seventeenth century, African slaves and European indentured servants worked together to build what Ira Berlin character-

---

3   Jan de Vries, *The Industrious Revolution* (New York: Cambridge University Press, 2008).

4   Sidney W. Mintz, *Sweetness and Power: The Place of Sugar in Modern History* (New York: Penguin Books, 1986).

izes as a "society with slaves" along the Chesapeake Bay.[5] These Africans were slaves, but before the end of the seventeenth century, they were not chattel, not fully. Planters and overseers didn't use them that differently than their indentured servants. Slaves and servants alike were subject to routine corporeal punishment. Slaves occupied the furthest point along a continuum of unequal and coercive labor relations.[6] Even so, 20 percent of the Africans brought into the Chesapeake before 1675 became free, and some of those freed even received the headright—a plot of land—that was promised to European indentures. Some of those free Africans would command white indentures and own African slaves.

To the British inhabitants of the Chesapeake, Africans looked different. They sounded different. They acted different. But that was true of the Irish, as well. Africans were pagans, but the kind of people who wound up indentured in the Chesapeake weren't exactly model Christians. European and African laborers worked, fornicated, fought, wept, birthed, ate, died, drank, danced, and traded with one another, and with the indigenous population. Neither laws nor customs set them apart.[7]

And this would become a problem.

By the 1670s, large landowners—some local planters, some absentees—began to consolidate plantations. This pushed the headrights out to the least productive lands on the frontier. In 1676, poor whites joined forces with those of African descent

---

5 Ira Berlin, *Many Thousands Gone: The First Two Centuries of Slavery in North America* (Cambridge, MA: Harvard University Press, 2000).

6 Russell R. Menard, *Migrants, Servants and Slaves: Unfree Labor in Colonial British America* (New York: Routledge, 2001).

7 Kathleen M. Brown, *Good Wives, Nasty Wenches, and Anxious Patriarchs: Gender, Race, and Power in Colonial Virginia* (Chapel Hill: The University of North Carolina Press, 2012).

under the leadership of Nathaniel Bacon. They torched James-town, the colony's capital. It took British troops several years to bring the Chesapeake under control.

Ultimately, planter elites thwarted class conflict by writing laws and by modeling and encouraging social practices that persuaded those with white skin to imagine that tremendous social significance—inherent difference and inferiority—lay underneath black skin.[8] New laws regulated social relations, and thereby actually created new social relations between the "races"—laws about sex, marriage, sociability, trade, assembly, religion.

The law of chattel applied to African and African-descended slaves to the fullest extent on eighteenth-century plantations. Under racialized chattel slavery, master-enslavers possessed the right to torture and maim, the right to kill, the right to rape, the right to alienate, and the right to own offspring—specifically, the offspring of the *female* slave. The exploitation of enslaved women's reproductive labor became a prerogative that masters shared with other white men. Any offspring resulting from rape increased the master's stock of capital.[9]

Global commerce in slaves and the commodities they produced gave rise to modern finance, to new industries, and to wage labor in the eighteenth century. Anchored in London, complex transatlantic networks of trading partnerships, insurers, and banks financed the trade in slaves and slave-produced commodities.[10]

---

8   Winthrop D. Jordan, *White Over Black: American Attitudes Towards the Negro, 1550–1812* (Chapel Hill: The University of North Carolina Press, 2013).

9   Jennifer L. Morgan, *Laboring Women: Reproduction and Gender in New World Slavery* (Philadelphia: University of Pennsylvania Press, 2004).

10   Stephanie E. Smallwood, *Saltwater Slavery: A Middle Passage from African to American Diaspora* (Cambridge, MA: Harvard University Press, 2008).

Merchant-financiers located in the seaports all around the Atlantic world provided a form of international currency by discounting the bills of exchange generated in the "triangular trade." These merchant-financiers connected British creditors to colonial planter-debtors. Some of the world's first financial derivatives—cotton futures contracts—traded on the Cotton Exchange in Liverpool. British industry blossomed. According to Eric Williams, the capital accumulated from the transatlantic trade in slaves and slave-produced commodities financed British sugar refining, rum distillation, metal-working, gun-making, cotton manufacture, transportation infrastructure, and even James Watt's steam engine.[11]

After the American Revolution, racialized chattel slavery appeared—to some—as inconsistent with the natural rights and liberties of man. Northern states emancipated their few enslaved residents. But more often racialized chattel slavery served as the negative referent that affirmed the freedom of white males.[12] In *Notes on the State of Virginia* (1785), Thomas Jefferson—who never freed his enslaved sister-in-law, the mother of his own children—postulated that skin color signaled immutable, inheritable inferiority:

> It is not their condition then, but nature, which has produced the distinction. . . . Blacks, whether originally a distinct race, or made distinct by time and circumstances, are inferior to the whites in the endowments both of body and mind. . . . This unfortunate difference of color, and perhaps of faculty, is a powerful obstacle to the emancipation of these people.[13]

11 Eric Williams, *Capitalism and Slavery* (Chapel Hill: The University of North Carolina Press, 1994).

12 Edmund S. Morgan, *American Slavery, American Freedom* (New York: W. W. Norton & Co., 1975).

13 Thomas Jefferson, *Notes On the State of Virginia,* Archive.org, March 8, 2010.

Even so, the former plantation colonies of the Upper South stood in a sorry state after independence, beset by plummeting commodity prices and depleted soils. After the introduction of the cotton gin in 1791, these master-enslavers found a market for their surplus slave-capital.

The expanding cotton frontier needed capital and the Upper South provided it. Racialized chattel slavery proved itself the most efficient way to produce the world's most important crop. The United States produced no cotton for export in 1790. In the antebellum period, it supplied most of the world's most-traded commodity, the key raw ingredient of the Industrial Revolution. Thanks to cotton, the country ranked as the world's largest economy on the eve of the Civil War.

From about 1790 until the Civil War, slave traders and enslavers chained one million Americans of African descent into coffles and marched or shipped them down to southeast and southwest states and territories. They were sold at auction houses located in every city in the greater Mississippi Valley.

Capital and capitalist constituted one another at auction. At auction, slaves were stripped and assaulted to judge their strength and their capacity to produce more capital or to gratify the sexual appetites of masters. Perceived markers of docility or defiance informed the imaginative, deeply social practice of valuing slave-capital. In this capital market, Walter Johnson reveals, slaves shaped their sale and masters bought their own selves.[14]

After auction, reconstituted coffles traveled ever deeper into the dark heart of the Cotton Kingdom and, after 1836, into

---

14 Walter Johnson, *Soul by Soul: Inside the Antebellum Slave Trade* (Cambridge, MA: Harvard University Press, 2001).

the new Republic of Texas.[15] Five times more slaves lived in the United States in 1861 than in 1790, despite the abolition of the transatlantic slave trade in 1808 and despite the high levels of infant mortality in the Cotton Kingdom. Slavery was no dying institution.

By 1820, the slave-labor camps that stretched west from South Carolina to Arkansas and south to the Gulf Coast allowed the United States to achieve dominance in the world market for cotton, the most crucial commodity of the Industrial Revolution.[16] At that date, U.S. cotton was the world's most widely traded commodity. Without those exports, the national economy as a whole could not acquire the goods and the credit it required from abroad.

And the Industrial Revolution that produced those goods depended absolutely on what Kenneth Pomeranz identifies as the "ghost acres" of the New World: those acres seeded, tended, and harvested by slaves of African descent.[17] Pomeranz estimates that if, in 1830, Great Britain had to grow *for itself, on its own soil* the calories that its workers consumed as sugar, or if it had to raise enough sheep to replace the cotton it imported from the United States, this would have required no less than an additional 25 million acres of land.

In New England and (mostly) Manchester, waged workers spun cotton thread that steam-powered mills spun into cloth. Once a luxury good, cotton cloth now radically transformed the way human beings across the globe outfitted themselves and their sur-

---

15 Walter Johnson, *River of Dark Dreams: Slavery and Empire in the Cotton Kingdom* (Cambridge, MA: Harvard University Press, 2013).

16 Brian Schoen, *The Fragile Fabric of Union* (Baltimore: John Hopkins University Press, 2009).

17 Kenneth Pomeranz, *The Great Divergence: China, Europe, and the Making of the Modern World Economy* (Princeton: Princeton University Press, 2000).

roundings. Manchester and Lowell discovered an enormous market in the same African-American slaves that grew, tended, and cleaned raw cotton, along with the same workers who operated the machines that spun and wove that cotton into cloth. According to Seth Rockman's forthcoming book, *Plantation Goods and the National Economy of Slavery,* the ready-made clothing industry emerged in response to the demand from planters for cheap garments to clothe their slaves.[18]

The explosion in cotton supply did not occur simply because more land came under cultivation. It came from increased productivity, as Ed Baptist illustrates.[19] The Cotton Kings combined the bullwhip with new methods of surveilling, measuring, and accounting for the productivity of the enslaved, radically reorganizing patterns of plantation labor. Planter-enslavers compelled their slave-capital to invent ways to increase their productivity—think of bidexterous Patsey in Solomon Northup's *Twelve Years a Slave.*[20] At the end of every day, the overseer weighed the pickings of each individual, chalking up the numbers on a slate. Results were compared to each individual's quota. Shortfalls were "settled" in lashes. Later the master copied those picking totals into his ledger and erased the slate (both mass-produced by burgeoning new industries up north). Then he set new quotas. And the quotas *always increased.* Between 1800 and 1860, productivity increases on established plantations matched the productivity increases of the workers that tended to the spinning machines in Manchester in the same period, according to Baptist.

18 Seth Rockman, "Implements correspondingly peculiar," Bard Graduate Center via YouTube, October 31, 2011.

19 Edward E. Baptist, *The Half Has Never Been Told: Slavery and the Making of American Capitalism* (New York: Basic Books, 2014).

20 Solomon Northup, *Twelve Years a Slave: Narrative of Solomon Northup, a Citizen of New York, Kidnapped in Washington City in 1841, and Rescued in 1853,* ed. by David Wilson (Chapel Hill: The University of North Carolina Press, 2011).

Slavery proved crucial in the emergence of American finance. Profits from commerce, finance, and insurance related to cotton and to slaves flowed to merchant-financiers located in New Orleans and mid-Atlantic port cities, including New York City, where a global financial center grew up on Wall Street.

Cotton Kings themselves devised financial innovations that channeled the savings of investors across the nation and Western Europe to the Mississippi Valley.[21] Cotton Kings, slave traders, and cotton merchants demanded vast amounts of credit to fund their ceaseless speculation and expansion.[22] Planter-enslavers held valuable, liquid collateral: two million slaves worth $2 billion, a third of the wealth owned by all U.S. citizens, according to Baptist. With the help of firms like Baring Brothers, Brown Brothers, and Rothschild, the Cotton Kings sold bonds to capitalize new banks from which they secured loans (pledging their slaves and land for collateral).[23] These bonds were secured by the full faith and credit of the state that chartered the bank. Even as northern states and European empires emancipated their own slaves, investors from these regions shared in the profits of the slave-labor camps in the Cotton Kingdom.

The Cotton Kings did something that neither Freddy, nor Fannie, nor any of the "too big to fail" banks managed to do. They secured an *explicit and total* government guarantee for their banks, placing taxpayers on the hook for interest and principal.

It all ended in the Panic of 1837, when the bubble in south

---

21 Edward E. Baptist and and Louis Hyman, "American finance grew on the back of slaves," *History News Network*, March 7, 2014.

22 Joshua D. Rothman, *Flush Times and Fever Dreams: A Story of Capitalism and Slavery in the Age of Jackson* (Athens, GA: University of Georgia Press, 2014).

23 Charles Rappleye, *Sons of Providence: The Brown Brothers, the Slave Trade, and the American Revolution* (New York: Simon & Schuster, 2007); Edward E. Baptist, "Toxic debt, liar loans, and securitized human beings," *Common-Place* 10, no. 3 (2010).

eastern land and slaves burst. Southern taxpayers refused to pay the debts of the planter-banks. Southern states defaulted on those bonds, hampering the South's ability to raise money through the securities markets for more than a century. Cotton Kings would become dependent *as individuals* on financial intermediaries tied to Wall Street, firms like Lehman Brothers (founded in Alabama).

It didn't take very long for the flow of credit to resume. By mid-century, racialized chattel slavery had built not only a wealthy and powerful South but it had also given rise to an industrializing and diversifying North.[24] In New England, where sharp Yankees once amassed profits by plying the transatlantic slave trade—and continued to profit by transporting slave-produced commodities and insuring the enslaved—new industries rose up alongside the textile mills. High protective tariffs on foreign manufacturers made the products of U.S. mills and factories competitive in domestic markets, especially in markets supplying plantations.

After the Erie Canal opened in 1824, the North slowly began to reorient towards timber and coal extraction, grain production, livestock, transportation construction, and the manufacture of a vast array of commodities for all manner of domestic and international markets. Chicago supplanted New Orleans.[25] By the 1850s, industrial and agricultural capitalists above the Mason-Dixon line no longer needed cotton to the same extent that they once did.[26] With the notable exception of Wall Street interests in New

24   Anne Farrow, Joel Lang and Jenifer Frank, *Complicity: How the North Promoted, Prolonged, and Profited from Slavery* (New York: Ballantine Books, 2005).

25   William Cronon, *Nature's Metropolis: Chicago and the Great West* (New York: W. W. Norton & Company, 1992).

26   Sven Beckert and Seth Rockman, "Partners in iniquity," *The New York Times,* April 2, 2011.

York City, Northerners began to resist the political power—and the territorial ambitions—of the Cotton Kings.[27] Sectional animosity set the stage for the Civil War.

But up to that point, slave-capital proved indispensable to the emergence of industrial capitalism and to the ascent of the United States as a global economic power.[28] Indeed, the violent dispossession of racialized chattel slaves from their labor, their bodies, and their families—not the enclosure of the commons identified by Karl Marx—set capitalism in motion and sustained capital accumulation for three centuries. [29]

Julia Ott is associate professor of history and director of the Robert L. Heilbroner Center for Capitalism Studies at the New School.

---

27 Sven Beckert, *The Monied Metropolis: New York City and the Consolidation of the American Bourgeoisie, 1850–1896* (New York: University Cambridge Press, 2001).

28 "15 major corporations you never knew profited from slavery," *Atlanta Black Star,* August 26, 2013.

29 Karl Marx, *Capital Volume I* (New York: Penguin Publishing Group, 1992).

Eric Anthamatten

Punching Nazis in the Face

A Philosopher Makes the Case for Violent Resistance

> "My human dignity lay in this punch to the jaw…"
> —Jean Améry, *At The Mind's Limits*

As white supremacist Richard Spencer was being interviewed on camera, a masked protester punched him square in the jaw. Many conservatives looked at this as evidence of "cry-baby" liberalism: when unable to handle alternative points of view, leftists resort to violence to stifle "free speech." This criticism has also been leveled against those who engaged in vandalism at the counter-inauguration protests and, more recently, at the University of California, Berkeley, protests of another alt-right personality, Milo Yiannopoulos (despite the fact that the "violence" was proportionately negligible, given the size of these events). Even some liberals, progressives, and leftists, while abhorring the neo-Nazi rhetoric of Spencer, would not go so far as to condone the violence against him or at these protests.

Fifty years ago, philosopher Jean Améry made a sustained argument for punching Nazis in the face, not only as an acceptable action, but one that might be required. A victim of torture by the Gestapo and a survivor of the Holocaust, Améry described his disturbing experience of torture at the hands of fascism, and defended, contra Nietzsche, the role of resentment (*ressentiment*) as an essential element of human identity, dignity, will, and freedom, including its manifestation in violence, as in the time he punched a Nazi in the face.

> I had grasped well that there are situations in life in which our body is our entire self and our entire fate. I was my body and nothing else: in hunger, in the blows that I suffered, in the blow that I dealt. My body, debilitated and crusted with filth was my calamity. My body, when it tensed to strikewas my physical and metaphysical dignity. In situations like mine, physical violence is the sole means for restoring a disjointed personality.

Punching the Nazi in the face was the only way that Améry could resist being reduced to a mere body, a passive object, a thing. He had to punch to restore the boundary between his personhood and the intrusion of the torture, the fascist, the racist: "The boundaries of my body are also the boundaries of myself. My skin surface shields me against the external world. If I am to have trust, I must feel on it only what I *want* to feel."

In some of the most difficult-to-stomach passages in all of philosophy, Améry describes his torture. His hands were cuffed behind his back and were raised to the ceiling by a chain. "The balls sprang from their sockets. My own body weight caused luxation; I fell into a void and now hung by my dislocated arms. . . . Torture, from Latin *torquere,* to twist." The effects of his torture went beyond the physical: his own body, the very thing that allowed him to be an "individual," the grounding of his freedom in the world, his most intimate "home," now became the source of pain, was no longer "his," but was now the weapon of the enemy.

Nor is Améry simply describing the harm visited upon him as an individual by the fists and sticks of the Gestapo. His scope is broader. In twisting the body, torture twists all of reality and "becomes the inversion of the whole social world." Torture wounds the flesh and the spirit, but also the very conditions of possibility that make our world human and all that the concept "human" entails—morality, creativity, sociality, and freedom. Torture annihilates humanity.

Torture is the essence of fascism. Fascism is the total control of all aspects of society—politics, economy, media—and in controlling these, controlling the bodies and minds of the individuals of that society. Historically, this has been tied to theories of racial purity and superiority. While it might be possible to imagine a fascist society that is not racist, to advocate ordering the world along racial lines is to advocate fascism. Racism destroys plurality, creativity, and freedom. Racism destroys the very idea of a "human individual." Racism twists and tortures the human world.

Are there situations, per Améry, where it is acceptable, even required, to punch another human being in the face? Even most pacifists, when pushed, will acknowledge that violence is acceptable in cases of self-defense, even where "self " can extend beyond the individual body or dignity to one's property, family, community, or society (this is precisely the purported rationale for most wars).

Améry's argument for Nazi face-punching isn't a version of the argument for self-defense, however. Crucially, he acknowledges that his punch was not only futile, but would lead to even more pain being inflicted upon him, perhaps even death. In this way, Améry's argument cannot be seen as a mere act of self-preservation, but as something that was demanded of him, as a human being, to preserve the integrity of the human world. His reasoning for Nazi-punching moves beyond ethical discourse into an ontological justification: what is at stake is not his individual body, but all of our bodies, and, perhaps, our world itself.

Perhaps Améry's and the protester's punches are significantly different: Améry having been a direct victim of torture; Améry having "nothing to lose"; Améry not punching in public under the gaze of cameras, running the risk of having the footage propagated and manipulated for various agendas, or, even worse, turned into a joke, thus diluting the image.

Another possible objection: "Sure, Richard Spencer propagates hate speech. Richard Spencer extends his arm in Nazi salute and says 'Hail Trump.' But he doesn't lynch people, or drop Zyklon B gas into a chamber. 'Sticks and stones.' Besides, if you think that torture and fascism destroy the human world, isn't punching someone in the face, even if that person is a hateful Nazi, doing the same thing?" (that these "critiques" often come from people— both conservative and liberal—that are secure in their bodies is no small point).

In fascism and racism, human bodies are on the line. To condemn punching Nazis in the face is to condemn anyone who fights back against violent assault. It is to ask them to give their bodies and their lives over to an abstract ideal of "free speech." It is to say that morality and reality exist on some ethereal plane, beyond faces and flesh and blood. It is, quite possibly, to accept the annihilation of the world itself.

A racist is not evil because he holds a certain set of beliefs or uses certain racist words. A racist is evil because he is part of a historical and systemic violence that does destroy people—economically, politically, psychically, and, all too often, physically (Richard Spencer advocates "peaceful ethnic cleansing"). The racist not only destroys individual minds and bodies, but makes it impossible to be at home in the world, much less to share this home with others. The racist turns the friend into the enemy, the neighbor into the stranger, and the brother and sister into an alien. By destroying these bonds, the racist annihilates humanity. The racist is an acolyte of death.

Maybe there are other, more effective ways to stand against the Richard Spencers and Milo Yiannopouloses of the world. But the two punches—that of the torturer and that of the tortured—are not equivalent, logically, morally, or otherwise. The first punch destroys. The second restores. The first punch is death. The second is life. The first punch is the enemy of humanity. The second punch is a friend, maybe even a hero, with the courage to confront the face of the enemy.

Postscript: *Améry writes that, "Whoever was tortured, stays tortured." Despite his great contributions to philosophy, he never was able to feel at home in the world again. In 1978, he committed suicide by overdosing on sleeping pills.*

Eric Anthamatten received his Ph.D. from The New School for Social Research in 2014, completing a dissertation titled "Habilitation and the Criminal: Punishment, Prisons, Pedagogy." He teaches at The New School and Fordham University. He also frequently teaches courses at the New York Public Library, free to the public, on various themes in philosophy.

About the editors

Chris Howard-Woods graduated from The New School in 2018 with a B.A. in philosophy. He previously served as media editor at *Public Seminar.*

Maryam Omidi is a graduate student in psychology at The New School, an editor at *Public Seminar,* and managing editor of the university's Publishing Initiative. She is a former journalist and author of *Holidays in Soviet Sanatoriums.*

Colin Laidley graduated from The New School in 2018 with an M.A. in Creative Publishing and Critical Journalism. He is an editor at *Public Seminar.*

From left to right: Colin Laidley, Maryam Omidi, and Christopher Howard-Woods
Photo by Preston Roberson-Charles